Praise for Martha Heller and
THE CIO PARADOX

"In *The CIO Paradox*, Martha Heller has clearly articulated the many contradictions that permeate the CIO role. But more than that, she includes rich examples of how successful CIOs have managed to break through these contradictions. IT leadership is a balancing act, as Heller demonstrates in this entertaining and insightful book."

—Carol Zierhoffer, VP & Global CIO, Xerox

"Martha does a great job of capturing the paradox of not just the CIO role, but of Enterprise IT as a whole. In a world that greatly admires technology and over-rewards the start-up, how is the "brand" of the enterprise CIO and the technology teams that support our business so weak? As a CIO who has survived this paradox for more than a decade, I appreciate the insights of *The CIO Paradox*."

—Robert B. Carter, EVP & CIO, FedEx Corporation

"In *The CIO Paradox*, Heller has her finger on the pulse of the major contradictions that plague the CIO role today, including being hired to be strategic, but spending most of our time being operational. Her recommendations on how to overcome major paradoxes offer concise and helpful advice to CIOs on becoming more successful in the role."

—Gregory S. Smith, author of *Straight to the Top:*
Becoming a World-Class CIO

"Martha Heller has unparalleled access to CIOs. She advises them, writes about them, and recruits them. With her terrific book, *The CIO Paradox*, she lets us in on all that she has learned and the advice she has given. The result is an invaluable resource. Martha demonstrates that for CIOs to be successful in this day and age, they must achieve balance in their skills, plans, and methods to eliminate blind spots and to achieve sustainable success for their departments and for their companies."

—Peter High, President, Metis Strategy, LLC and author of
World Class IT: Why Businesses Succeed When IT Triumphs

"What makes *The CIO Paradox* a compelling read is the understanding Martha has of the vast challenges today's CIOs are faced with. Throughout the book you have those "aha!" moments that energize any reader who works in or supports the IT profession. The organized, blunt fashion in which she states the paradox, while injecting the perfect amount of humor, is terrific, as are her conclusions. This is not a book about IT that will bore you!

—Pamela J. Stenson, SVP & General Manager,
CIO Executive Council

"A must-read for all CIOs and those aspiring to the role. *The CIO Paradox* is a compendium of our colleagues' most valuable and sometimes painful lessons packaged up and told in a compelling and straightforward manner. Heller has distilled years of CIO experience into a pragmatic guide that not only helps CIOs everywhere to improve their game, but forces them to reflect on where they have been and, more importantly, where they should go next."

—Timothy C. McCabe, SVP & CIO, Delphi

"Martha Heller has captured the essence of the exhilaration and the stress that come with being a CIO in the 21st century. In *The CIO Paradox*, she has articulated the complex and critical set of issues that confront CIOs every day, in every enterprise, in a witty and constructive way. Having lived the CIO role over four different decades, I was able to relate to her paradoxes and her assertion that to be successful in this young and great profession you must move from being an "either, or" manager to an "and, and" leader. It will be exciting to see more and more of our next generation leaders break through these paradoxes."

—Charlie Feld, Founder, The Feld Group Institute, and author of
*Blind Spot IT: A Leader's Guide To IT-Enabled
Business Transformation*

THE
CIO
PARADOX

THE
CIO
PARADOX

Battling the Contradictions
of IT Leadership

MARTHA HELLER

bibliomotion
books + media

First published by Bibliomotion, Inc.

33 Manchester Road
Brookline, MA 02446
Tel: 617-934-2427
www.bibliomotion.com

Printed in the United States of America

ISBN 978-1-937134-27-3

Library of Congress Cataloging-in-Publication Data

Heller, Martha.
    The CIO paradox : battling the contradictions of it leadership / Martha Heller.
        p. cm.
    Includes bibliographical references and index.
    ISBN 978-1-937134-27-3 (alk. paper)—ISBN 978-1-937134-28-0 (ebk.)—
ISBN 978-1-937134-29-7 (enhanced ebk.)
    1. Chief information officers.   2. Information technology—Management.   I. Title.
    HD30.2.H46 2012
    658.4'038—dc23
                        2012032981

For Mom and Dad

Acknowledgments

It takes a village to write a book. My husband, Tony Vaver, has had to deal with my waking up in the middle night yelling, "Book? Who said I could write a book? What was I thinking?" A published author himself, Tony has the uncanny ability to get me over my author anxiety (which often means applying just the right amount of red wine to the situation). Tony knows how to talk me down, and for that, I am eternally grateful.

My daughters, Maddy and Audrey, are the apple of my eye. Despite the fact that they tended to roll their eyes when I mentioned "The CIO Paradox," they always let me have my writing space and entertained me during my breaks.

Honestly, I don't know where I would be without all of my friends at CXO Media. Rick Pastore has been an editorial mentor to me for many years. As he has done so many times before, Rick helped me to take a germ of an idea and turn it into a bona fide framework with editorial legs. Maryfran Johnson, who wrote the Foreword to this book, has been a friend and partner to me since the day we met. Her gentle critique of my onstage presence has made me a better speaker. Pam Stenson is a source of great inspiration to me. She has built the CIO Executive Council into a thriving business and has provided me with many wonderful opportunities to connect with the CIOs in her considerable networks. Diane Frank, my *CIO* magazine column editor, turns a pig's ear into a sow's purse every month, and Carrie Mathews, who directs the CIO Executive Council's web conference series, has welcomed me onto her digital stage.

As for my colleagues at Heller Search, I cannot believe my good fortune in being allowed to work with the best executive search team in the business. Carol Lynn Thistle, my director of recruiting, joined me in launching Heller Search Associates when we had nothing more than basements and cell phones. Carol Lynn has been a superb partner to me and has taught me more about retained search than I have taught her about anything. Steve Rovniak, Pam Kurko, and Katie Fichera dazzle me daily with their work ethic, smarts, and collegiality. They raise the bar on my own performance and make every day at Heller Search a good one.

Jill Friedlander, Erika Heilman, Jill Schoenhaut, and Susan Lauzau, my publishing team at Bibliomotion, have been exceptional every step of the way (even during my temper tantrums). Rusty Shelton has provided us with great vision when it comes to social media.

And let's not forget the CIOs. For the last thirteen years, busy CIOs have allowed me to force my way onto their calendars. They have been so generous with their time, stories and insights that I have no idea how to repay them. Hopefully, this book is a drop in that cavernous bucket.

Finally, I would like to thank Cynthia, Steven, Justin, Ruth, Jason, and Alison for all of the good times. This has been a tough few years for the Heller children, and the way we have supported each other would have made our parents proud.

Foreword

By the time I met Martha Heller in the fall of 2006, I'd been hearing her name bandied about for years. *CIO* magazine's Founder and CEO Joe Levy had regaled me with tales of this entrepreneurial, business-savvy editor who was helping him launch a new CIO professional association.

That venture eventually blossomed into our CIO Executive Council (one of our magazine's most successful startups ever), as Martha sailed off into a new career as an executive recruiter.

"You should meet Martha," Joe kept saying. "You'll really get along." I suspect he was thinking I could learn a thing or two about business acumen from her, but he was too much of a gentleman to say so. Journalists tend to live on the outer banks of the revenue stream, where making money is (alas) one of the last things on our minds.

So there I was, moderating a luncheon panel of Boston-area CIOs, and the time had come for audience Q&A. This is a dreaded moment for moderators, handing over control of that microphone. (What if nobody has a question? They've been awfully quiet so far.) I was also aware that 95 percent of IT executive audiences are serious introverts. Public speaking is about as appealing to them as snake-handling.

Thankfully, the curly-headed, commanding presence who rose to her feet that day was Martha. "We have a question at our table. Well, actually, we have several," she said, getting an immediate laugh as she took over the room and kept the conversation moving. I met a kindred spirit that day—someone who loves talking to CIOs and hearing their stories every bit as much as I do.

Whenever I'm tempted to call Martha the "CIO Whisperer" (for she does have the ear of the IT leadership community nationwide), I remember she never needs a microphone to make herself heard. Whispering is not one of her core skills.

We've been colleagues and friends ever since that long-ago panel discussion, trading CIO contacts, story ideas, career advice (and fashion tips about stage-worthy outfits). A few months after I took over as *CIO*'s editor in chief in 2009, Martha's CIO Paradox column made its debut in our magazine.

Readers were so responsive and engaged with her ideas that we cleverly realized how well the CIO Paradox would work on stage at our events. The other half of my magazine job is creating and running a dozen CIO conferences during the year. I'm constantly filling "pages and stages" with CIOs and their stories, so I take advantage of Martha's talents as a speaker whenever I can lure her away from her day job. We believe those face-to-face sessions with CIO audiences across the country have continued to refine this fascinating topic.

Simply put, the CIO paradox is a hot mess of contradictions built right into the CIO role.

This is the only C-suite-level job regularly declared to be on the verge of extinction. You don't hear many debates about whether CEOs or any of the other chiefs (of finance, HR, marketing, operations) have a future. Yet everybody seems to have something dire to predict about where CIOs are heading.

One of the great ironies of the trillion-dollar information technology industry is how eager the vendors are to sidestep the head of technology and sell directly to the heads of marketing or sales (those titans of IT operational knowledge). That's even more likely to happen now in this latest tech bubble around cloud computing, consumer mobile devices and social collaboration tools.

Now that we can all point-and-click our way to what looks like IT expertise, who needs CIOs and IT departments?

I take comfort in the fact that these imminent-CIO-demise theories have been hanging around like ants at a picnic since our magazine's first issue in 1987. Yet here we are, more dependent on technology than ever, paradoxically convinced that any random business executive can do a better job than a CIO. Business people don't understand how IT works, so they fear it, resent it and dismiss it. Then they hire consultants for some expensive talk therapy about why they should fire the CIO.

As Heather Campbell, former CIO of Canadian Pacific Railway, lightly observes in the chapter on the accountability vs. ownership paradox: "My former boss used to say, 'There are only two types of projects: business successes and IT failures.'"

What Martha has accomplished with this timely, wonderfully written book brings the whole paradox conversation to a higher level—one where you'll find detailed ideas, wise advice and specific answers from the accomplished CIOs who have managed to break through various parts of the blockade.

You'll notice that these paradoxes have a rabbit-like ability to multiply, so she corrals them into four major sections dealing with your role, your business stakeholders, your staff, and your future. Each chapter flows around multiple conversations with CIOs about the real business problems they solved, and ends with an instructive summary and bulleted list of the most actionable pieces of advice. Some of it will seem oh-so-familiar to you, but the first-person stories breathe new life into old adages about leadership, communication and change management.

At Boeing Corp., for example, CIO Kim Hammonds set out to sharpen some of the blurry lines between IT and engineering, which over the years had grown used to running its own technology operations. "It's a balancing act that we walk every day," she says. "We cannot stop the engineers from making technology decisions, but we need to get in there to make sure the IT content is protected, secure, and efficient."

CIOs often tell me that they come to our executive conferences hoping to go home with just one or two new things to think about. A hallway conversation with someone can spark the creative thought pattern that later solves some completely unrelated problem. You'll find many such sparks in *The CIO Paradox*.

Unlike other business books, you (mercifully) won't find 12-step programs, magic quadrants, or tediously detailed frameworks. Instead, you'll read a lot of memorable, well-spun tales. You'll hear directly from CIOs like Geir Ramleth of Bechtel, who realized that IT gets a (justifiably) bad name with the other employees because "we always come up with complexities and barriers...we overlook the simplest solution."

To break his own complexity paradox, Ramleth created a formula to inspire his IT organization to think differently: Speed = Innovation × Simplicity. "If we can build a very simple organization, we should be able to react to business change quickly," he notes.

You'll hear how CIOs like Daniel Priest of Toyota Financial Services struggle to manage the flood of ideas from sales and marketing teams about serving the digital consumer. You'll learn why CIO Michelle Garvey of Warnaco devotes extra time to monitoring the company "buzz" during major transformation initiatives. ("You need to understand the noise—what people are saying about a project.") You'll see why CIO Mike Capone of ADP credits his rotational experience through other business units for his ongoing success. ("I lived on the other side of the equation and saw firsthand how IT impacted my business.")

One of the paradoxes I find the most maddening to address is that infamous "IT and the Business" divide (peacefully laid to rest in chapter 5). Although IT is embedded in every aspect of business, it's often seen as a separate (but unequal) entity, a thing apart from the mainstream of the company. CEOs are notoriously uncomfortable with technology and tend to marginalize it, so CIOs end up obsessing about IT/business alignment.

"We may have a seat at the table, but we have not gotten as close to the table as heads of HR and finance," as CIO Colleen Wolf of Ventura Foods explains it. "Salespeople understand finance, and finance people understand HR, but no one fully understands what IT actually does. So we are on an island."

Building a bridge from that island to the business mainland is a complex task requiring a long list of relationship-building leadership skills. Many of those attributes find their way into the final chapter's "Breaking the Paradox Checklist," which includes some unexpected advice about cultivating patience and growing your own IT/business "blended" executives.

Martha's own blended background as a journalist-turned-recruiter gives her a deeper, more nuanced understanding of IT leaders and the problems they're trying to solve. The many great anecdotes and contributions from well-respected CIOs are a genuine testimony to her extensive network of interview sources, friends, colleagues and clients. But in the end, it is her story-telling talents and sparkling sense of humor ("like weight loss and world peace, solving the CIO Paradox is a journey") that makes reading *The CIO Paradox* such a pleasure and a worthwhile investment of your time.

Maryfran Johnson
Editor in Chief, *CIO* magazine & Events

Contents

PART IV
YOUR FUTURE: WHAT'S NEXT FOR THE CIO?

What Is the CIO Paradox?

In 1999, I started asking CIOs a question: *When you walked into your most recent CIO job, what did you find?* The answer was almost always the same: "I inherited a mess. IT had no credibility with the business. Projects were overdue and over budget. We had no project management discipline, no governance, no career paths, and the team had outdated skills." Thirteen years later, I am still asking the question, and I am getting the same response at the same rate. CIOs continue to inherit a mess.

How can this be? How can CIOs strive tirelessly to improve their IT organizations only to leave "a mess" in their wake? Why has the rate of failure of IT projects and IT organizations remained so high over the years? Why are we still talking about "IT value" and "alignment" and "getting a seat at the table"? Why do CIOs still work harder than most of their executive peers to establish credibility? Is every CIO I have ever known an idiot? (Most of them seem pretty smart to me.) Is it just human nature to trash what has come before us? (Probably, but that cannot explain the pervasiveness of the issue.) Or is there something so inherently problematic about the CIO role that even talented, intelligent, and experienced leaders have trouble making it work?

In the late 90s, I joined *CIO* magazine as a writer, then launched and ran a number of programs for CIOs including the CIO Best Practice Exchange and the CIO Executive Council. As an executive recruiter, I have recruited CIOs for almost every major industry and have helped CIOs build out their own leadership teams. As a result of all this experience, I know hundreds and hundreds of CIOs. You would think that I would be able to come up with an answer to my burning question of why CIOs almost always inherit a mess. But not only have I failed to develop a viable answer, I have come up with more questions:

- Why is it that CIOs devote significant energy to succession planning, and yet when they leave, their CEOs typically go outside to replace them?
- Why is it that IT can be a company's strategic differentiator—or can bring a company to its knees—yet corporate boards rarely appoint CIOs?
- Why do CEOs claim they are seeking a strategic IT leader, yet a year later, the new CIO winds up spending all of her time putting out operational fires?
- Why does IT leadership get harder as the business community gets smarter about technology?
- Why do companies still not know how to hire a CIO?

After pondering these questions for far too long (I do have a life, you know!), I finally reached a conclusion: there is something deeply, foundationally, problematic about:

- Our personal relationship to technology and our reliance on it for productivity;
- The discomfort that most senior executives have with subjects (like technology) that they do not understand;
- The conflicting timelines between technology deployment and business change;

- The conflicting timelines between large IT implementations and technology innovation in the market place;
- And the sheer complexity of technology.

These problems, I believe, result in a CIO Paradox: a set of perennial contradictions that permeates the core of the CIO role. Some CIOs buckle under the CIO Paradox and struggle against it in their jobs every day. But successful CIOs—the ones who no longer worry about alignment and credibility and reporting structure and getting a seat at the table—have found a way to deal with the Paradox. One way or another, they have learned to manage the contradictions of the job.

When I came up with this CIO Paradox idea a few years ago, I was so delighted by it that I called up my friend and colleague Rick Pastore, vice president of editorial and programs at the CIO Executive Council, and took him to lunch. I presented my idea and, as Rick typically does, he helped me beat it into submission. He suggested that I write a new "CIO Paradox" column for *CIO* magazine, and in December 2009, I introduced the CIO Paradox to *CIO* magazine readers. I have been writing about it ever since.

Rick and I divided the CIO Paradox into four categories (which became the basis of a CIO Paradox poster we also produced).

Your Role

- You were hired to be strategic, but spend most of your time on operational issues.
- You are the steward of risk mitigation and cost containment, yet you are expected to innovate.
- You are seen as a service provider, yet you are expected to be a business driver.
- IT can make or break a company, but CIOs rarely sit on corporate boards.

Your Stakeholders

- You run one of the most pervasive, critical functions, yet you must prove your value constantly.
- Your many successes are invisible; your few mistakes are highly visible.
- You are intimately involved in every facet of the business, but you are considered separate and removed from it.
- You are accountable for project success, but the business has project ownership.

Your Organization

- Your staff is most comfortable with technology, but must be good with people.
- Your staff is doing more with less, but must make time for learning finance and the business.
- You develop successors, yet the CEO almost always goes outside to find the next CIO.
- You are forced to seek cost-efficient overseas sourcing, yet you are expected to ensure the profession's development at home.

Your Industry

- Technology takes a long time to implement, yet your tool set changes constantly.
- Technology is a long-term investment, but the company thinks in quarters.
- Your tools cost a fortune, yet they have the highest defect rate of any product.
- You sign vendors' checks, yet they often go around you and sell to your business peers.

My dear friends Maryfran Johnson, editor-in-chief of *CIO* magazine, and Pam Stenson, general manager of the CIO Executive Council thought there was enough to the idea of the CIO Paradox that they let me onstage at their conferences (not knowing, of course, the dangers of giving me a microphone) and allowed me to talk through the paradox with CIOs across the country.

The reaction to the CIO Paradox was mixed. Some people felt I was giving voice to their deepest thoughts about their role and told us they hung our CIO Paradox poster on their office wall. Others politely suggested that I stop facilitating the mass whining of the CIO population and let everyone look up from their navels long enough to get back to work. (I did notice, however, that even the most critical CIOs suggested a paradox or two of their own that they thought I should add to the list.) But whatever the reaction, I found that the CIO Paradox created considerable discourse among CIOs about how they do their jobs. By breaking the role into its most paradoxical elements, CIOs got to the heart of what makes their job so demanding and began sharing advice, challenges, and lessons learned that they had picked up from years on the job.

This book is structured along the same lines as the original set of CIO Paradoxes that Rick and I produced in early 2010. While most of the paradoxes on the original list rear their heads at some point in the book, I have refined and restructured a bit, and even added a few, having had the last two years to test the paradox out on my CIO networks.

The first section, Your Role: You're Damned If You Do, and You're Damned If You Don't, takes a hard look at the CIO position. I chose to lead with the Cost versus Innovation Paradox, because our current era of big data, mobility, and cloud computing gives CIOs the opportunity (and the challenge) to drive some serious innovation in their companies. But the demand for innovation doesn't decrease the need for cost efficiencies. Innovation ain't cheap, and neither is technology.

Chapter 2 addresses the paradox that CIOs tend to find most vexing. It is the tension between strategy and operations and the balancing act that CIOs—and their teams—must walk between them. In chapter 3 we take on

The Global Paradox and focus specifically on the leadership challenges that face CIOs who run sprawling organizations that span multiple time zones.

In Part 2, Will the Business Ever Love IT?, we begin with the Archivist versus Futurist Paradox, which we can also call the Legacy Paradox, if we like. As one CIO said to me recently, "Legacy begins the day you put something in," which is a challenging situation if ever there were one. I personally find this paradox to be one of the more fascinating, and it is only getting more intense in our current computing paradigm. In chapter 5, we discuss the fact that there continues to be, in so many companies, a clear divide between "the business" and "IT." This chapter will probably upset you. You will be annoyed that we are still having this discussion, and you will probably wonder why I was ever allowed to set pen to paper. But if you can contain your rage for long enough, I feel confident that you will pick up a few good tips on how to bring the business and IT together. In the last chapter of the section, which covers the Accountability versus Ownership Paradox, we hear how CIOs make good on the claim that "in my company there are no IT projects, only business projects."

In Part 3, we discuss Your Staff, because where would you be without your team? I have entitled this section "They Just Don't Make Them Like That" for a reason. As someone who has been recruiting your directors and VPs for many years, I have in-the-trenches knowledge about how the CIO Paradox manifests in up-and-coming IT professionals. Those gorgeously blended high-potentials who have business and technology and leadership and interpersonal skills are out there, but they aren't growing on trees. If you are good at recruiting them and growing your own, you will win the war on talent that seems to have snuck up on us again. If you are not, you will lose.

In this section, we first look at the methods CIO's use to recruit from the outside. This chapter is my plea to all of you to examine and improve your recruiting practices. In chapter 8, we explore the Enterprise Architecture Paradox, because enterprise architecture, I believe, is the most paradoxical of all of your senior positions. Finally, we address the CIO

Successor Paradox with an eye toward improving your ability to populate the world with great future CIOs.

The final section, What's Next for the CIO?, begins with a chapter about CIOs and corporate boards. Board directorship is an attractive final frontier for CIOs who have had successful careers, but those gigs are tough to get. We'll hear from two CIOs who have served on corporate boards about how they made it happen. In the following chapter, we will expand on some of the ideas that I explored in the "Life after CIO" series that I wrote when I was *CIO* magazine's Career Strategist columnist in the late 2000s. That series, and this chapter, discuss pathways out of the CIO role, for those so inclined. And the last chapter acknowledges that we are currently at an inflection point, where the "technology productization" of so many business models in so many companies is sure to have an impact on the future of the CIO role. Will the person sitting in your chair ten years from now do your job the way you do it today? I doubt it.

In the conclusion (and don't you *dare* skip right to it), we group together in one long list the impressive array of attributes and skills that successful CIOs all seem to bring to their roles, regardless of the particular paradox they are battling. I call this the Breaking the Paradox Checklist.

What has truly amazed me during the many years that I have been working with the CIO community is the wealth of knowledge that CIOs possess and their generosity in sharing it with one another. I have not come across another professional group that turns so consistently to its peer networks for information and guidance. My approach to writing this book stems from that same rich tradition of peer information exchange. I set up interviews with CIOs from a wide range of industries, threw a few paradoxes out on the table, and asked about their approaches to managing them. I took the comments I believed would be most valuable to a readership of IT leaders and built my chapters around them.

I want to be clear that this book is not a step-by-step guide to solving the CIO Paradox. It does not provide a single model for overcoming all of the challenges CIOs face. The very nature of the CIO Paradox would never allow for such a thing. The keys to solving the CIO Paradox lie in the experiences, thoughts, lessons learned, philosophies, wit, and wisdom of all of those CIOs who are actually doing these jobs. I will leave the multi-tiered road maps and seven-step models to the consultants who know more about running IT than I do. That is not my thing. My thing is facilitating peer information exchange.

In 2000, when I worked for CIO.com, I launched an online community called "The CIO Best Practice Exchange." Thousands of CIOs logged in and participated in discussions about almost every facet of IT leadership. What resulted was a rich repository of content about IT leadership from executives on the front lines. Gary Beach, publisher of *CIO* magazine at the time, suggested I take the show on the road and conduct "Best Practice Exchange" panels at *CIO's* executive events. Those panels became the foundation for what is now the CIO Executive Council, a global professional community and another powerful example of peer information exchange.

My goal is to position this book squarely in the tradition of CIOs sharing information with each other. My role as writer is—as it has always been—to dig for and report on the secret sauce that makes CIOs successful, and to present it in the same tone as CIOs sharing tips over coffee at a conference.

In the chapters that follow, we will explore the many facets of the CIO Paradox and hear from CIOs who have found a way around them. We will introduce the concept of "breaking the paradox," that is, establishing yourself as a CIO who no longer worries about getting a seat at the table, and talking in the language of the business, and all of the other things that CIOs spend hours at conferences discussing. We will learn the approaches CIOs take toward establishing a platform where they enjoy a high level of credibility, and where they are considered, at all layers of the organization, to be superior executives who have made their companies stronger. But just like weight loss and world peace, solving the CIO Paradox is a journey. It is my sincere hope that this book helps you make your own journey a success. Enjoy!

PART I

Your Role: You're Damned If You Do and You're Damned If You Don't

1

The Cost versus Innovation Paradox

I was talking recently with the CIO of a pharmaceutical company, who told me that one drug can cost more than $4 billion to produce. I found that number to be a tad bit staggering, so I asked him to explain. He told me that the R&D group puts a large number of drugs into production at one time because the team knows that most of the drugs will fail at some point in the R&D process. The one drug that does survive will more than compensate for the R&D costs, so the overall budget allows for all of that failure. In order to innovate, pharmaceutical executives figure, they need to build waste and failure into their process.

That got me thinking about CIOs and the imperative they face to drive innovation while at the same time keeping the infrastructure secure and efficient. When was the last time you had extra budget for waste and failure? When was the last time you could focus all of your attention on innovation and take your eye off security and cost management? Pharmaceutical CIO Maurizio Laudisa describes the situation very well: "CIOs must look at risk with a pragmatic lens, which is sometimes viewed as contrary to creativity and innovation. The cost of artistic creativity is often complexity and error; our delivery mandate can afford neither of those."[1] Or as Kim Hammonds, CIO of aerospace giant Boeing, puts it, "Our job is to figure out how to stabilize the 'run' side of the business and then take those cost savings and reinvest them in the innovation side of the business." The CIO Paradox to which they refer is, of course: *As CIO, you are the steward of cost containment, yet you must also innovate.*

Werner Boeing, CIO of Roche Diagnostics, sees the Cost versus Innovation Paradox as a fairly recent phenomenon. "We are in the midst of universal change from an 'either cost or new features' model to an 'And' philosophy, where we need to do both," he says. "CIOs who have traditionally defined their accountability in terms of technology delivery will need to adjust. It is no longer enough to deliver on IT projects in a cost-effective way. The new 'And' philosophy expects you to have full accountability for the business outcomes of IT, cost effectiveness *and* innovation, including areas where you do not have direct control."[2]

For the last thirty years, the twin goals of IT have been efficiency and productivity, and the CIO's role has been to make everything faster and cheaper. When businesses were run on spreadsheets, IT could put in a few software systems and deliver some pretty significant value. With the advent of e-mail and other collaboration tools, IT kept on delivering. Along came ERP (enterprise resource planning), and CIOs became involved with business process change, which helped them continue, for the most part, to deliver on IT's promises. Enter outsourcing, and CIOs had another productivity arrow in their quiver.

Cloud, consumerization, and mobility have moved CIOs into a new zone and have created a new set of responsibilities and business expectations. According to Werner Boeing, "When it comes to consumer technologies, many CIOs have not found a way to define their contribution in this new environment, and the business perceives us as standing in their way. Our traditional mantra of standardization and consolidation does not work anymore." In other words, those CIOs who are spending their time writing policies about whether or not employees can use iPads at work are missing the point. "Many CIOs believe that simply orchestrating the consumerization trend is their role and that giving people a work experience similar to the one they have at home is a valuable contribution. But that's not innovation, that's just deploying technology," says Boeing.

If CIOs can no longer provide enough business value through consolidation, standardization, business process change, and deploying iPads at work, where should they focus? "The new dimension for IT contribution is business model innovation," says Boeing. "It is about giving up the defensive stance and being an active driver in changing the way your company does business. Business model innovation is the new contribution of IT."

Be a Chameleon

If CIOs are to adopt and deliver on a new mantra of business model innovation, they have to reassess the skills they bring to the job. "Here's a paradox for you," says Boeing. "People believe that IT is about technology, but it's really a behavioral science—understanding the behaviors of your company's staff, leaders, and customers—and facilitating the adoption of a new vision."

So, your mission, if you choose to accept it, is to view IT innovation not as project delivery, change management, and business process reengineering, but as setting a vision for business model innovation. It's not "How can I deliver iPads to my sales team?" but "How does the advent of iPads change our business model, and how can I share that vision with my fellow executives?"

Now, this is a tall order indeed. CIOs are already responsible for internal systems, data management, business process change at an enterprise level, and the security and deployment of thousands of new devices. Let's add meeting with external customers, developing new business models for the company, and communicating the vision for new models to the company at multiple levels. According to John Dick, CIO of HR consulting firm, Towers Watson, probably the most important skill a CIO can possess is the ability to do it all, to move from operations to security to project oversight to innovation, as business needs and technology options change. I call this ability to adapt "the chameleon factor," and it is not a skill that everyone possesses.

Naturally, a paradox comes to mind. The "DNA" necessary to write code and configure networks and do many of the technology-oriented tasks that today's CIOs performed in the early stages of their careers is entirely different from the DNA necessary to see the future and make others see it too. Some CIOs simply do not have the chameleon factor that allows them to move from project delivery to business model innovation. These CIOs should establish firm footing for themselves as operational leaders and leave the business model innovation to other executives. Other CIOs have the gene for innovation, but they are working for CEOs who refuse to recognize IT's potential to innovate. If these CIOs cannot change the hearts and minds of their executive peers, they would be better off finding a company more excited about IT innovation.

Develop a Really Effective Metaphor

CIOs who have the chameleon factor—and are working for companies ripe for innovation—will need to develop new ways to communicate the multifaceted role of IT. Here is where a good metaphor can come in handy. CIOs have always loved metaphors—those wonderful spaces where two parties with different backgrounds can get closer to a shared understanding of something complex and abstract. If you don't have a good metaphor to explain IT's new role in efficiency and innovation, you should probably develop one. Werner Boeing provides a great example. When Boeing began his role as head of IT for Roche Diagnostics in 2010, the mantra of the IT organization was globalization. "In the absence of real business cases, globalization was their charge," says Boeing. "But globalization should never be a strategy. It is a structure in support of something else." So Boeing needed to replace globalization as a strategy with a new model for what IT was all about, something that covered operations, business process change, and the newest goal of the IT organization: innovation.

"How does one organization ensure secure and standardized operations in a regulated environment, allow the business to work more effectively, and create space for people to experiment all at the same time?" wondered Boeing. He brainstormed with a photographer about the best way to articulate this three-pronged mandate in one image: he was looking for an image that obliterated the Cost versus Innovation Paradox.

Boeing and his photographer settled on a photo of a particular crossroads in Spain that had one lane populated by huge trucks, one lane with taxis moving through it, and one lane with motorcycles. "The lanes represent the three different modes of IT operations within one global organization," says Boeing. The trucks represent accepted, foundational, and unchanging truths about the business that apply at a global level and are typically delivered through bigger programs. "Certain things are set in stone throughout the entire company," says Boeing. "What is our material master? What is a customer? What is a vendor? These are global concepts. Don't waste our time questioning them."

The taxi lane represents projects that are delivering business processes that are not standardized on a global level and which might be treated differently in different regions and business units. "Take customer relationship management," says Boeing. "In one country, we might use a basic sales force automation tool, because of the level of maturity of that market, and in another, we might build a sophisticated and highly integrated solution for the entire region, because its markets are more mature or more complex." The taxi lane represents standardization, but it has more flexibility than the truck lane. "With the taxis, we are not coming in with a global hammer. It is all about the right timing and sequencing."

The motorcycle lane is all about innovation through pilots and experiments. "If we want more taxis, we need to create a meaningful space for safe experiments," says Boeing. "Let's not govern everything to death. If you have a good idea, try it out in the right lane with the right effort." The ideal flow, over time, moves from motorcycle to taxi to truck. "The more processes we can move from motorbikes to taxis to trucks, the more we are bringing innovation right into the core of our business," says Boeing.

"When I joined the company, we had a traffic jam. We were global when it came to the technology platform, but we hadn't thought through how to manage our processes on a global basis, and we were not innovating enough," says Boeing. Using the crossroads metaphor, Boeing is able to illustrate the course for an organization, strategy, and road map that will allow IT to reduce costs and drive innovation at the same time.

For example, Boeing and his executive colleagues have taken the concept of "commercial excellence" out of the truck lane—where commercial excellence was led at a global level by a global governance body—and put it into the taxi lane, "because market conditions and how excellence is defined are different from region to region," he says. Using the crossroads metaphor, Boeing and his colleagues have also been able to introduce speedy motorcycles like ad hoc services for business partner collaboration via SaaS. And they have cleared out a traffic jam in the taxi lane through a global prioritization program that moved some global business functions over to the truck lane.

"IT resources are limited, so we can only absorb so many new projects at a given time," says Boeing. "The crossroads metaphor illustrates that IT projects are all about managing dynamic traffic patterns where we can keep operations running and create short-term space for innovation."

Keep it Simple

Like Werner Boeing, Geir Ramleth, CIO of engineering giant Bechtel Group, sees the perennial tension between innovation and cost as recently becoming more acute. "IT originated in companies through osmosis," Ramleth says. "We came in to support department issues like payroll, inventory, and order taking, and wound up with MIS directors for each of those organizations running isolated systems. We almost had a data center per department." Once managers had their individual departmental issues solved, they wanted to integrate processes end to end, and IT stepped in.

"We started tying the departments together for an enterprise view; bought software, like ERPs, from other people, and we put in relational databases," says Ramleth. "And the environment shifted from a terminal to a desk computer to a laptop." We are now going through yet another paradigm shift where IT's accountability has extended well beyond the enterprise. "You come to the world of cloud and consumerization, where we are solving value chain issues by tying separate enterprises together in environments where the processes extend beyond our reach," says Ramleth, "where information is no longer tied to applications, where the information generated in one enterprise might show up on a totally different system in another enterprise, and internal relational databases are no longer sufficient."

As a result of this paradigm shift, CIOs who have spent years learning to strike the fine balance between innovation, delivery, cost, and risk have to figure it out all over again. "We have shifted over time from central to de-central, and lately to a 'universal' environment where my work environment is no longer my desk-based terminal, desktop or laptop; it is actually my identity, which I can take to multiple devices. But we still need to deliver," says Ramleth. "That is the paradox I am fighting right now. How do you paint an airplane while it is flying?"

When Ramleth took over as CIO of Bechtel in 2002, he found what so many CIOs discover when they join a new company: IT cost way too much for what it was delivering "One of our most senior executives told me, 'I don't know what you do, but you cost too much'," he says. "When I first heard that, I was really mad. If you don't know what you're buying, how can you judge the price? But then I thought it through, I realized that what he was really saying was, 'I don't want to get into how you are doing what you're doing, but I am not happy with the impact.'"

So Ramleth and his team started measuring the gross cost of IT on a global basis, and divided it by the company's output, with the goal of reducing the cost of IT per output unit, a single work hour. "Today, that number is down 63 percent over what it was ten years ago." Clearly, Ramleth was able to improve the operational side of the equation, but he also needed to keep the innovation coming.

Simplify

According to Ramleth, "One of the reasons IT often gets such a bad name with other employees is that we always come up with complexities and barriers for what we want to do and we overlook the simplest solution." To combat that tendency, Ramleth came up with a formula: Speed = Innovation × Simplicity. He used this formula as a beacon for his IT organization. "Innovation, I can pretty much get from other people, so all I need to do is provide simplicity, which is where we'll get 80 percent of the payback. If we can build a very simple organization, we should be able to react to business change quickly."

He started by standardizing functions and processes on a global basis. "When I came on board, we had thirty-three different help desks around the world. So, we built one global 24-7 help desk system with one ticketing system on one phone number, which we could distribute around the world. We put the entire function under one manager. We increased the number of problems we solve on the first call from 20 percent to over 65 percent and took costs down by more than 30 percent," Ramleth says.

Likewise, Ramleth and his team reduced the company's data centers first from twenty-seven to seven, then later down to three. "With all of our data center operations under one manager, we are able to collect standardized metrics. When your results are measurable, and no longer anecdotal, you are able to improve your speed of change dramatically."

Use that simplicity to embed innovation in your organization

Many CIOs, including several I interviewed for this book, carve out an innovation group filled with those brilliant technologists who have a flair for business and the insight to predict which emerging technologies will provide the most bang for the buck. At Bechtel, Ramleth takes a different approach. "I don't believe in having a separate innovation group. In that scenario, those people come back with proposals for major change, and they can become very disruptive," he says. "We embed innovation into our existing operations. That way, you get innovation, speed, and cost advantages all at the same time."

By standardizing functions and processes across the many countries in which Bechtel operates, Ramleth finds that his global organization is able to strike a good balance between innovation and cost. "When you take away the complexity and simplify what you have around the world, you wind up with what we call global leverage platforms, which you can use to push change or innovation through very effectively," he says.

Eighty percent is good enough

Several years ago, Ramleth and his team were rolling out a set of systems to support construction projects that Bechtel had around the globe. The systems worked everywhere except in one remote desert region; this region was home to a major project but it also suffered from extreme network latency. "At first, we tried to engineer our overall global solution so that it would work everywhere including for this one project," says Ramleth. "But we realized that it would take forever to figure that out, and by designing for the lowest common denominator, we were dragging everyone else down. So we said, 'let's stop thinking that we have to solve the infinite problem. Let's build the solution for the rest of the company and find something else that will work for the desert location.'"

Use newer companies, like Google, as your benchmark

Rather than look to other 110-year-old, $30 billion global enterprises, which are all fighting the same battles, Ramleth and his team take a different approach. "Let's go analyze the companies that had the privilege of starting in the last ten years and figure what they are doing," he says. "Our benchmark shouldn't be the best in our industry; it should be the best of breed regardless of industry."

Ramleth and his team found that companies born in the post-Internet era gave them a view into simplicity that older companies did not. For example, Ramleth built simplicity into Bechtel's mobility strategy by studying Netflix and Google. "We decided that, rather than try to get consumer products in our enterprise environment, we would find a way to adapt our enterprise environment for consumer products," Ramleth says. "We developed an open-based API strategy where applications go to get relevant information. We can now write consumer-like applications that can access the information securely, both internally and externally. If I want to get SAP information on my iPad, I don't try to get the full native SAP application to run on my iPad; I try to figure out how to get the information I want from SAP into a native iPad application. That way, we simplify how our applications work effectively with the back-end core systems, and actually increase security. We have simplified and reduced the overall application interaction as every transaction gets authenticated, authorized, and accounted for."

Ramleth's simple API solution paved the way for more speed and innovation. For example, he and his team researched the way Bechtel's knowledge workers used information and found that 80 percent of them only read information, rather than adding, editing, or deleting a record from an application or database. "Eighty percent of our information workers wouldn't learn our applications. Instead they requested a report delivered by e-mail," says Ramleth. "When we were developing a business intelligence strategy, which can be such a large up-front investment, we decided to run small specialized applications through our API system. We used these small applications to produce targeted information, which we could then use to create 'mash-ups,' or composites, out of which we could get real knowledge. When we began to change our view of our users from contributors of information to consumers who just want a small sliver of data, the world became very simple. We found that we could innovate without much cost."

Reorganize for Innovation

Tom Farrah became CIO of Dr Pepper Snapple Group soon after Cadbury Schweppes spun off the beverage company in 2008. He and his team had a long way to go—and a lot of integration ahead of them—before they could start driving innovation. In 2006, the company had acquired its largest independent bottler, which was itself made up of thirty newly acquired bottlers, amounting to an integration plan that included ten separate ERPs, thirty different route accounting systems, and multiple flavors of mainframe systems.

Once the Dr Pepper Snapple Group's IT team had integrated the bottling business, they moved on to their distribution centers and warehouses, which they merged into the same environment. Finally, they standardized onto one handheld system for field workers. "This is what we did for three years," says Farrah, "but we knew that the integration would not grow top-line revenue and market share. We were no longer content to sit back and say, 'Driving revenue has nothing to do with us. We can't control how much you sell.'"

After Farrah had finished the integration, he had to change the culture of the organization to focus on innovation. "How do I change my IT organization's mentality from asking 'How do I deliver my projects' to 'How do I attack the real issues that handcuff the business and prevent the company from selling more product?'" he says.

Farrah's first step was to outsource. "Once we had the infrastructure integrated and stabilized, we started outsourcing most of the day-to-day operations," says Farrah. "Now that our internal people are no longer spending their days on help desk tickets, they are able to work on our innovation tracks, like mobility and business intelligence."

Make your relationship managers accountable for innovation

Next, Farrah had to reorganize IT: "Even before we started our integration program, we had set up the organization with innovation in mind," he says. Farrah structured the group around directors who are accountable for a given stakeholder group, such as finance or national accounts. These directors are mini CIOs accountable both for delivery of day-to-day service and for Farrah's innovation tracks. So, how does Farrah ensure that his directors strike the operational and innovation balance?

"When we were a part of Cadbury, we had created roles called relationship managers, but these people didn't own the delivery," he says. "We still had central groups for development and infrastructure. So you had these relationship managers whose job was to interface and manage demand, but they were handcuffed because they didn't own any of it."

At Dr Pepper Snapple, Farrah has changed the model so that the director, who is thoroughly embedded in the business and engaged in strategic discussions, also owns delivery. Farrah still has a few shared service delivery people for networking and telecom, but the accountability for IT innovation, strategy, and delivery lies completely with the IT director, not with the shared services group. "Before, the relationship managers would go to the business, understand the demand, and bring it back to the larger teams, which would create the project or systems enhancement or whatever. But those larger teams, which had this really rigid structure, would own and manage the delivery and execution." The poor, embattled relationship managers were stuck in the middle, with little control and without the credibility to participate fully in strategy discussions. In the new model, because the directors own the delivery, they are able to turn innovation into value at a much more rapid pace.

Create an innovation group

While at Bechtel, Geir Ramleth has chosen not to carve out a separate group for innovation, many CIOs do. Twila Day, CIO of Sysco, the $39 billion food service supplier, was having a hard time bringing new technology ideas to the business, so she pulled together a small group of IT people into a research group. Their mandate is to look at new technologies and processes and how they might apply to the company. "We have a lot of people who keep the lights on," says Day. "So if we don't make innovation somebody's job, it will be pushed to the side." Day cautions that in setting up an innovation group, you do not simply select your most productive or senior leaders. "You have to make sure that your group is made of people who can work with less structure than what most IT positions require," she says. "They have to be creative in their thinking." Day also advises that you resist the urge to lay too many rules or structure on the group. "You need to give them the leeway to look at technology investments in new ways," she says. "ROI comes in different flavors; you may need to accept some failures along the way," she says. "That is the hardest thing for many organizations who hate to waste money. With innovation, sometimes you have to stub your toe."

Build a Culture of Innovation

In 2006, Tom Conophy became CIO of InterContinental Hotels Group (IHG), which operates more than 4,100 properties in more than one hundred countries. He walked into an IT organization "that was striving for mediocrity," he says. "It had been disenfranchised from the business and was not considered a group to look to for consultation or guidance. This was the classic scenario of an organization that had the capability but was in the wrong mind-set."

Conophy did three things simultaneously. "First, I started engaging with all of the different business owners to learn the good, the bad, and the ugly as it related to IT's ability to support the business's needs. Second, I started to address operational issues and stabilize the environment, and third, I began to engage with the IT organization and assess the capabilities of the team."

Conophy put together a SWAT team to get a handle on the cause of some major systems outages and began to stabilize the infrastructure. In the process, it became clear to him that he had to change the culture of the IT organization so that it was more focused on innovation.

I want to pause here and say a word or two about the need for CIOs to drive cultural change, as it is probably the most critical aspect of the job, whether that cultural change takes place directly in the IT organization or across the company. There is a paradox at the center of the quest for cultural change. If you asked a random employee which organization embodies your company's culture, what would she say? Marketing? Customer Service? Sales? I'll bet you my entire shoe collection she wouldn't say IT. As we will discuss in chapter 5, in many companies, IT is considered something outside the business. (In some companies, it is so far removed from the heart of the business that it is housed in a separate building.) Yet when you look at companies that have undergone massive cultural transformation, which department do you think was a major driver of that change? IT! This is a critical theme I discovered while conducting my interviews for this book: IT is so costly, complex, and integrated into every aspect of the company that the IT organization typically excels at disciplines like budget management, strategic planning, project management, continuous improvement, and leadership development. The most successful CIOs (the ones who have broken the paradox) are those who do more than apply IT to business problems. CIOs who have broken the paradox take the expertise they have developed in their role as leaders of the IT department and use it to make improvements across the enterprise. They are company leaders, in addition to being IT leaders. We'll see this theme emerge throughout the book, and we'll address it again in the concluding chapter.

Back to Conophy. In his first week on the job, he was meeting with a group of two hundred people from data center operations to talk through metrics and SLAs and uptime and change control processes, and after listening to the discussion for about ten minutes, he interrupted: "I did this Black Panther thing where I stood up and said, 'I didn't come here to strive for mediocrity! Who's with me?' I threw my fist in the air, and while I certainly shocked some of the people, I actually got others on their feet."

Conophy knew from his discussions with the CEO and the board that he had a strong mandate to change IT, "so I needed to break some glass and get the team to take some risks," he says. Once he got the team's attention and made the declaration that the time for change was now, Conophy needed to put his money where his mouth was and start solidifying the new mind-set through symbols and programs.

Change the mission statement

Conophy says, "Very early on, I started reviewing some basic questions with the technology leadership group like: 'What is our core purpose? What is our mission? What are the principles and tenets that we believe in? How are we going to behave?' We printed our mission on these eight-and-a-half-by-eleven laminated cards that we basically showed to everyone," he says. Conophy still has a few of those cards, which read: *Our mission is to transform technology to be the enabler of brand differentiation.* "That became our mission for more than six years," he says.

Change the physical environment

Conophy ripped out all of the traditional conference room furniture and replaced big tables with small tables that the teams could configure the way they wanted. He painted the department with bright colors and installed floor-to-ceiling whiteboards, power cords, and stereo systems everywhere. He named meeting rooms after famous computer scientists and built open spaces furnished with beanbag chairs and "love seats and sofas and all that stuff," along with foosball tables and Wii games. And he provided free sodas and snacks. "The facilities people pushed back on the free sodas, arguing that 'If we do free soda for your team, that means we have to do free soda for everybody,'" Conophy recounts. "So we said, 'That's too damned bad, we're going to do it,' and we put our own machine, with free sodas, right next to the pay machines that were already there." It may well be that a couch is a couch and a soda is a soda, but when technologists feel like they are working for Google, they have an easier time getting into an innovative frame of mind.

Conophy also built what he called "caves." He told the team, "If you're into it, we've got this lab where you can set up some equipment to try something new, you know, do some experimentation, knock yourself out." The caves concept led to two technology patents for IHG's IT department. Conophy notes, "For the last sixty years, our company had one patent, and in the last five years, we've generated three others, two of which came from the caves. Both patents are critical components of IHG's e-commerce experience and core reservation platform."

Start a CIO fund

Early on, Conophy negotiated an investment of $1 million in capital and $500,000 in operating costs to fund innovation. "It was a budgetary place holder I used to fund out-of-the-box ideas," he says. A person on Conophy's staff had an idea about modifying one of the company's major systems. "So, I gave him a little bit of money and some time to work on that," says Conophy. "He went into the cave and started working through the algorithms. We bought some additional equipment to let him test his theories, and then we let him run it in parallel for a period of time."

That innovation became a formal initiative that led to the deployment of a patented technology called BOSS, or Bottom-Up Optimumized Search Strategy, a Java application that runs on an Oracle RAC database and allows for a reversal of the traditional top-down search approach. "IHG runs more than fifty-two million hotel availability transactions a day, and all of it is being served by BOSS," says Conophy.

Give a little money to enterprise architecture

When Heather Campbell was CIO of Canadian Pacific Railway, she gave her enterprise architect $1 million for R&D, an amount that represented a small percentage of her overall budget. "One million dollars doesn't sound like a lot," says Campbell, who is now a president at consulting firm, BasicallyIT. "But my architect was used to having nothing. He had been in miserly mode for so long, it was actually a challenge to get him to spend the money." But Campbell's architect did spend the money, year after year, and the incubator he created produced some major innovation. "Through that R&D effort, we churned out iPads across the enterprise and gave our employees the ability to choose their favorite device. That initial investment was how we got into using the public cloud for application development. What we were also able to do through our little $1 million is figure out how to use the private cloud to re-platform all of our servers. We planned to reduce our data center costs by over 50 percent," she says.

Change your meetings

Once a year at InterContinental Hotels Group, Tom Conophy would bring together his senior technical team, roughly ninety people he called "The Jammers," for a "Tech Jam," a deep-dive meeting focused on technology. "Tech Jams are akin to Apple's or Microsoft's conference every year, where you are getting into code and talking about how things really work," he says. "These meetings were phenomenal. It was almost a cult thing in my organization."

What I find so interesting about Conophy's approach to building innovation into the IT organization is that, while he respected the corporate culture at IGH, he didn't worry too much about matching IT's culture with it. "IHG is a very conservative, traditional English corporation," says Conophy. "We couldn't go in that direction with our technical groups or we would never attract the right talent. Instead, we modeled the culture in our IT organization after what you would find in technology companies. That's the talent we were competing for."

Conophy's Tech Jams were nothing like the meetings that go on in the other functional groups at IHG. How could they be? Most IT people are technologists; they need to work with technology, to touch technology, to walk and talk technology—at least some of the time. CIOs spend so much time making sure their technologists are business people first and that they blend in around the table, to the point where they hang their heads in mortal embarrassment when one of their colleagues dares to utter a technical term in a business meeting. You have to remember that technologists are different, and if you squash that difference, you stand to lose some of their brilliance.

Surely this is one of the most enduring CIO Paradoxes of all time: *Technologists must be really different and just like everyone else, all at the same time.* As you strive to build innovation into your operations, you will need to find a way to let your technologists be technologists. How else will they think out of the box?

Conclusion

As CIO, you need to save money and spend money at the same time. You need to be both risk averse and a risk taker. You need simultaneously to look "down and in" and "up and out." You need to say "Not on my watch" and "By all means! Let's do it!" all at once. And you need to build a team that can balance these dichotomies.

In this chapter, we have heard a number of strategies for striking the cost versus innovation balance, but a few approaches CIOs use to break this particular paradox stand out:

- *Simplicity.* The need for CIOs to drive innovation will only increase over the next few years. The more complexity you can take out of your organization and your infrastructure, the faster you can deliver the *new* new thing.
- *Eighty percent is good enough:* Don't try to find the solution that will work in every single scenario for every single customer. Sure, most CIOs are programmed to solve every problem, but sometimes good enough is plenty.
- *Focus your team on innovation:* Your people know how to run a cost-effective infrastructure; that is in their comfort zone. Innovation is their next frontier. Whether you tear down walls, given your architects seed money, or pull people into a separate group, your team needs to hear the mantra of innovation ringing from the rooftops.
- *Find new ways to communicate:* For many companies, IT is not ERP anymore. It is new revenue and new customers and new ways of doing business. If your executive peers do not understand IT's new role, you need to find a new set of metaphors and other communication vehicles to show them the light.
- *Be a chameleon:* As IT changes from business process change to business model innovation, so must you. Over the next few years, your skills, vision, and perspective will need to shift from support to reinvention. This isn't the first time you've had to change up your skill set. You've done it before and you can do it again.

2

The Operations versus Strategy Paradox

For much of 2010, the good people at *CIO* magazine allowed me to lurk around their conferences, talking with attendees and placing our CIO Paradox poster on their tables. The poster listed our original set of sixteen CIO Paradoxes, and I asked CIOs to circle the three that resonated most deeply for them. Many of them chuckled knowingly at the paradox *"Your many successes are invisible but your few mistakes are highly visible"* and stifled a grimace at *"You sign vendors' checks but they often go around you to sell to your business peers."* But the paradox *"You were hired to be strategic but you spend most of your time on operational issues"* really struck a nerve. It ranked in the top three of the nearly four hundred CIOs I spoke with.

Why is this paradox so vexing to CIOs? For Ray Barnard, CIO of Fluor Corporation, one major factor behind the operations versus strategy challenge falls squarely on the shoulders of CIOs themselves. "CIOs have a tendency to believe that they are an overhead function," says Barnard. "When you believe you're an overhead function you operate differently than when you perceive yourself as leading a P&L. As an overhead functional leader, you get too caught up in day-to-day scenarios." But much of

IT is about day-to-day operations, and it is critical that those operations run well. How do CIOs who have grown up attuned to operational excellence broaden their perspective?

Deliver Revenue

When Barnard joined Fluor in 2002, "It was very obvious that CIO was a functional, overhead position," he says. He knew that he had to do something to change that perception. "I did an assessment of all of my suppliers and thought about how I could help put some business deals together," Barnard says. He made a list of twenty current and potential Fluor customers—companies where he knew the CIO or CFO—and he laid out a sales strategy for each of these companies: "I went to the executive vice president of sales and marketing and said, 'This is my plan. Do you want to assign a salesperson to me, or should I just go ahead and see what I can do?'" The EVP gave Barnard the go-ahead to call on his contacts, and within eighteen months he had helped position several billion dollars'-worth of deals, none of which had anything to do with IT.

"CIOs spend half their lives going to conferences," says Barnard. "If you have CIO relationships, why can't you turn them into revenue for the company?" After his successful foray into driving new revenue, Barnard was promoted to the senior executive level and considered a bona fide member of the executive team.

Kim Hammonds, CIO of Boeing, provides another example of how a CIO can drive revenue for her business. "I was recently at a session with twenty-five CIOs from the airline industry, and I talked to them about mobile security and some of the work we are doing in that area," she says. "That has generated a lot of interest from these customers because they are looking for help in securing their mobile devices. I don't cultivate great sales and marketing skills in my team, because sales and marketing are happening at each of the business units. But we can use our knowledge to educate our external customers on what we know about mobile security. We are solving it at Boeing, and we can help our external customers with the same challenges."

Do you have relationships that could be beneficial to your company but that have little to do with IT management? Have you thought about your network as a source of new business for your company? Can you approach your next CIO conference with an eye toward new revenue, as well as an opportunity to learn new ways to run IT? You are well on your way to breaking the CIO Paradox when your company perceives you as a revenue driver. And once you are known for driving new business, you are much better positioned to break all of those other CIO Paradoxes, as well.

Structure Your Organization for Strategy

You may be able to shift your own perspective from "all operations all the time," but if you do not change the way you run your organization, that shift will be short lived.

Tie your budget to the business

CIOs who have inherited the "overhead" mind-set from being immersed in traditional IT organizations over the years have to work hard to "think P&L." As an important step, Barnard suggests changing your cost structure from an allocation measurement to a recovery measurement. "I work on the basis of recoveries," he says. "As the business does well, I get specific recoveries, and those recoveries come back to me to pay for what I'm doing. If the business isn't doing well then I'm not getting my recoveries, and it drives me to different investment decisions, just as if I were running a P&L." Barnard sits down with every one of his managers each week and reviews the P&L status of each. "They show me what they've spent and how much they've recovered," he says. "That process has my team thinking more like a P&L as well."

Carve out your revenue driving teams

In addition to having some teams focused on running IT operations and others focused on application development, Boeing's Hammonds has 10 percent of her team (which amounts to eight hundred out of her eight-thousand-person IT organization) working on specific customer contracts. "Whether it is with the army, navy, or Department of Defense, we have teams that are focused directly on revenue-generating work," says Hammonds. That doesn't make Hammonds' organization a profit center. "We are still a cost center, but we are driving revenue flow to the business units." Hammonds has been very deliberate about carving out these contract-focused IT teams. "I have learned from past experience that there needs to be some separation between operations and strategic work," she says. "Because otherwise, people are so consumed with the running of the business that they can never focus on the future."

Have a solid IT roadmap process

Four years ago, Sysco CIO Twila Day implemented a roadmap process that she credits with keeping her IT organization focused on strategy. "When you are not constantly looking for new strategic opportunities, you have a tendency to get stagnant," she says. When Day and her team built their first IT roadmap, they discovered a disconnect between the projects on the roadmap and what the business wanted to fund. As a result, they made two major changes. "We engaged a third party to help us stay unbiased," she says. "If you try to run the process internally, you may wind up biased about what you are hearing from the business, because you have your own opinions about what the solutions should be." Day also participated in Sysco's corporate strategy group as a senior executive. "The strategy group is out working with the business, and I get to sit in on those update meetings and know what the top strategy projects are for the corporation," she says. Day's participation on the corporate strategy committee ensures a strong tie back to the IT roadmap process.

Manage your own expectations

While it would be great fun to spend all of your time on vision and strategy and new revenue and innovation, so much of IT is operational, that attempting to move the dial to strategy too quickly will only end in heartbreak.

Understand that operational excellence is strategic

"If you think that you are going to create a fifty-fifty balance between operations and strategy, then you are a fool," says Kevin Horner, who recently retired as CIO of Alcoa. "How much time you spend on each is something that you determine with your boss and the company's leadership when you walk in the door and probably again after ninety days. But if you can't strike the balance by the 101st day, that day should be your last."

When the recession hit Alcoa hard in September 2008, Horner responded by cutting 30 percent of his spend for the following twenty-four months. "The commodity side of the company lost two-thirds of its revenue in a five-month time frame, so we took every dime out of innovation and product costs and put it toward the bottom line. That was a strategic move," Horner says. "But I told the executive team that that strategy would not be sustainable for long and we would be coming back in 2011 for a major ERP investment."

Get smart before you get strategic

If your new CIO job is in the industry where you've spent your entire career, you can probably move into strategy work quite quickly. This has not always been the case for Kumud Kalia, who, having been CIO for

Dresdner Group North America, Qwest, Direct Energy, and now Akamai Technologies, has walked into new industries at several points during his career. "If you don't have industry experience, you have to pay your dues before you can make a strategic contribution," Kalia says. "You have to show that you really understand the business environment before you can expect people to give credence to your ideas. If I'm CIO of a product company and I don't understand our legacy—the evolution of our products, what's worked in the past, the history of customer satisfaction, how can I offer up ideas about the future?"

As CIO of Akamai Technologies, which is in an industry that is new to him, Kalia spent several months learning the company's history but also getting trained on its current operations. He learned how the company sells its products, how the products are priced and contracted, what kinds of problems customers have when they call support, and how new ideas get into project innovation. "I'm examining everything close up," he says. "I am learning what screens our customer service people look at and what kinds of conversations they are having. Once you've delved into the details, you have earned the right to talk with the CEO about how to run the business better."

Assess your own skills

Before he moved into IT, Kalia spent a part of his career as a consultant, developing business strategies for clients. "Strategy work relies on certain structures and models, and, like anything, unless you are trained to do it, it can be challenging, particularly if it is not a natural strength," he says. If you are great at operations, but strategy does not come naturally, you have to accept that and build complementary strengths on your team. "Hire a head of strategy or build linkages to your company's strategy team," says Kalia. "Not every CIO is strategic."

Be sure the company is ready for IT strategy

Another reason CIOs get stuck on operational issues, according to Fluor's Ray Barnard, is that the company perceives IT as a support function and is incapable of changing that bias. "If the company's leadership views IT as a cost center, you many never get out of the weeds," he says. "If that is the case, you may as well report to the CFO and maintain operations, because it's out of your hands." While Barnard acknowledges that there are many CIOs who have changed the perception of IT at their companies, just as he has done at Fluor, if the operational perception is old enough or deep enough, change may be too much of an uphill battle. In instances where IT is entrenched as an operations function and there is resistance to changing that approach, you would be better off working elsewhere.

Ask some questions and find out about the company's view of the CIO role before accepting your next job. "First, I would look to see where the position reports," says Barnard. "Second, I would see whether the position has a seat at the table with the CEO." Barnard also advises caution if interviewers spend 90 percent of their time asking about how you can save the company money. "Be careful of scenarios where the company has a big SAP problem that they cannot seem to solve. That's the sign of a company that looks at their CIO as overhead," he says. Barnard would rather see interviewers engage a CIO candidate in discussions about decisions on whether to structure the company on a regional or enterprise model. "That's indication that the CIO will have a chance to contribute to the corporation as a whole rather than just manage costs," he says.

Get Good at the Core; Get Rid of the Context (A Turnaround Story)

For Ron Kifer, CIO at Applied Materials, there are a number of contributing factors to the Operations versus Strategy Paradox but "the biggest is the fact that it is really tough to be strategic when your pants are on fire," he says. "The majority of CIOs are pretty much facing the same situation: a legacy of years of underinvestment in IT and poorly integrated applications." With approximately 80 percent of the IT budget going toward maintenance, "the bulk of their time, money, and talent are not focused on business-enabling change leadership," says Kifer.

We live in a society where the dominant ideology is that we are better off in the present than we were in the past. In 2012, we have anesthesia, polio vaccines, food processors, hybrid cars, flat screen TVs, and iPads. Progress is good, and we are living better than the poor suckers who preceded us. The same goes, one might expect, for the CIO role. Surely, now that you have learned from the mistakes of the CIOs who set up those legacy systems, you are in a better place. Now that your business peers have learned to love technology and all that it can do for them, you can shake off your budget woes of the past and assume your rightful position of strategic influence. With history as a guide, you can correct the sins of IT underinvestment and leave your house in better shape than you found it. But like most ideologies, the "I am better off than the CIO who came before me" mindset has its deficiencies. When it comes to the ability to shift IT spend from operations to strategic initiatives, most CIOs are no better off than their predecessors.

"The majority of the transformation models out there require significant incremental spend and long time lines to accomplish transformation," says Kifer. "Neither of those is typically available to CIOs with shrinking budgets and increasing expectations around immediate gratification. You are not going to get budget increases; you are not going to get three years to accomplish a transformation. Mobility, globalization, all of these things add layers of complexity and new problems that organizations simply did not have to face before. So as quickly as you resolve some of the basic blocking and tackling for the way things were, you now have to face a whole new paradigm."

In some ways, CIOs are indeed better off than they were a generation ago. The business, for the most part, understands that technology enables business success. But the strategic demands on CIOs are much greater than they used to be; we have only scratched the surface on all that mobility can do for businesses, and those demands are bound to get greater over the next few years. CIOs who have not managed to find better, cheaper ways to run IT operations, thus freeing themselves up to focus on new mobility strategies, for example, are going to get crushed.

My typical response, when I am caught between a rock and a hard place, is to complain bitterly and then drink a lot of red wine. (It isn't very pleasant; just ask my husband.) Ron Kifer suggests an alternate approach for getting out of the Operations versus Strategy Paradox. "You need to find a way to manage those things that are contextual or commodity in nature so that you can really focus on those things that are critical core competencies," he says. "I think that's what differentiates strategic from nonstrategic IT organizations." In other words, you and your IT organization have so much to do, and the list gets bigger every day, that you cannot go it alone. You need to figure out what activities you are really good at—and that no one else can do as well—and what activities someone else can manage for you. Sounds simple, right? It's just outsourcing. But outsourcing gone wrong can bring real suffering to an IT organization, and it happens all the time. When my firm is brought in to recruit a CIO, high on the list of candidate requirements is the need to "fix our broken outsourcing relationship."

Kifer has served as CIO of DHL Express Europe and of DHL's Rest of World organization. He has also held IT leadership positions with the California State Automobile Association, 4CS, Oregon Department of

Revenue, and Raytheon. In 2006, he joined Applied Materials, a $9.5 billion semiconductor maker.

For years, Applied Materials had delegated IT management to a rotating group of internal business executives, so hiring Kifer represented a real change for the company: he was the company's first professional CIO, he had an impressive CIO track record, and he was brought in from the outside.

Applied Materials had a solid reason for hiring Kifer. The company had a sparse corporate IT function with seventeen different IT groups, all of which reported into their respective business leaders and had no accountability to the corporate function. The CIO position reported into finance, several layers away from the CEO. The IT budget was a 90/10 split between run and build, and the company's M&A growth strategy was not supported by a concomitant technology integration strategy. The IT organization had no standards for project, program, or portfolio management (nor had the business, for that matter) and had not participated in any certification programs in its basic technical domains. More than half the IT staff was on contract, and they were employed by more than twenty different firms.

Guess what the perception of IT was in the rest of the business? It was great! IT enjoyed a tremendous amount of respect and credibility, and everyone loved working with them. (I am employing a literary device here, known as *sarcasm*, to make sure you are paying attention.) In reality, the business perceived IT as order takers who did not add a whole lot of value to the business.

In the midst of the dysfunctional IT environment Kifer inherited, the company was about to begin an end-to-end SAP implementation as part of a program to reengineer business processes across every business domain.

Ron Kifer's mandate was not insignificant. He was expected to lower costs, improve delivery, establish transparency, execute perfectly, and, while he was at it, change the culture of the IT organization and improve its relationship with the rest of the business. And he needed to create a way for this IT transformation to fund itself. Surely, this was an opportunity for Kifer to get stuck in the weeds.

Kifer's challenge, while formidable, is not entirely unique. As CIO, you have certainly been in a similar situation, where you are expected to produce miracles on a shoestring and in a short period of time. The fact is that most CIOs, at some point in their careers, inherit something so messy that the best description is "turnaround." But because the turnaround is so intense and the expectations are so high, the new CIO tends to stay focused on operations as the weeds grow around his ankles. And he never gets out.

In this scenario, a few years pass and the executive committee finds itself frustrated by a lack of forward-looking IT strategy, and an executive recruiter gets the call: "Our CIO is an order taker and is not adding any value; find us a new one." Kifer, who managed to avoid this sad but too-common tale, shares his approach to staying strategic while at the same time leading a massive and potentially "weedy" operational transformation.

Start the turnaround during your interview

Here's a fairly common phenomenon: During their interviews, CIO candidates talk about vision and growth and innovation and strategy with the executive committee, and everyone is happy and excited. One lucky CIO is awarded the job and then, a few months after he starts, he informs the executive committee that he has done an in-depth assessment, and has discovered that the infrastructure is in rough shape and in need of some major improvements. Everyone is annoyed, frustrated, and nervous about the big-ticket investment required for the turnaround, and the CIO has already failed at expectations management.

"If you wait for your first day on the job to begin the process of developing your transformation strategy, you may find that the train has left the station without you," says Kifer, who put his success criteria on the table during his interviews. He had four requirements that had to be met before he would accept the job, and he made sure those requirements were included in his acceptance letter.

First, he had to report to the CEO. Not only would that give him direct access to the CEO, it would also send a clear message to the organization that IT was changing its status at the company. Second, the CIO would be a peer to the other executives on the senior leadership team. "This gave me complete freedom to build the relationships necessary for a successful transformation," he says. Third, "We had an agreement that I would consolidate all of IT within the company very rapidly," a decision that meant that Kifer did not have to negotiate with sixteen business leaders to assume leadership of their IT organizations. The IT teams were his from day one. "If it doesn't report to you and you don't control the budget, you can't change it," he says. Finally, Kifer received a free hand to form the new leadership team within IT. Head count, hiring, and a shift from the heavily contract-based model were entirely within his control. "These conditions were nonnegotiable," says Kifer, who was prepared to walk away if he was unable to secure them.

We all talk about "executive sponsorship" and "CEO support." Those are pretty words, and they are fun to say, but they don't always happen once the transformation gets off the ground. By putting his demands right into his offer letter, Kifer sent a clear message that CEO support was not a nice-to-have. But even with his preconditions met, Kifer could have failed if he didn't anchor that support in a solid plan.

Develop your plan before Day One

Getting your operational house in order while also developing a strategic vision for the future is kind of like looking down and up at the same time, a paradox if ever there were one. To resist the pull of the weeds, Kifer suggests putting a strategy in place before you even start the job.

Before his first day at Applied Materials, Kifer began to outline a ninety-day plan to "identify those high-touch, high-visibility, quick wins in the organization to garner support for the really demanding change that would follow," he says. His first thirty days would be focused on building key relationships, and his plan included individual strategies for each senior executive, with clear deliverables, along with an assessment of the IT organization.

The sixty-day plan identified the key strategic elements necessary to achieve the vision, and quick wins, like single sign-on, remote access, spam management, and automated e-mail management, to get the stakeholders to stay with him during the much tougher change ahead. In this phase, Kifer planned an organizational model that would allow him to meet his cost-cutting goals and start building core competencies into his team. He would also build new models for budget and governance during this phase.

Finally, his ninety-day plan was all about execution: staffing plans, process documents, team assignments, and project schedules.

Identify what is context and outsource it

Probably the most important element of Kifer's transformational plan— and the key to allowing the organization both to operate and be strategic from the outset—was establishing an enterprise-managed services model and consolidating the twenty-plus IT service providers into a dual-vendor, long-term strategic relationship. "Our goal was to identify all contextual activities being performed in every functional area of the enterprise and migrate these over time to our managed service partners," he says. By outsourcing the context, Kifer was able to focus his team on their core competencies, "while taking advantage of the more mature processes, tools, and metrics of our service providers."

Don't make assumptions about context

Before you even show up for work as a new CIO, you can probably guess 90 percent of what is going to be context and what will be core. "But you need to remember that, in many cases, one organization's context is another organization's core," says Kifer. At some companies, for example, supporting remote workers is a nice thing to do, but it does not create a competitive advantage. But at Applied Materials, the ability for the company's engineers to be able to work at home seamlessly was critical to the company's overall R&D efforts. At Applied Materials, the remote working environment was a differentiator.

Once Kifer and his team decided to outsource such contextual functions as desktop, applications, network, and e-mail support, they needed to develop IT's core competencies, the most important of which were the three Ps (project, program, and portfolio management) and vendor management.

Improve all three "Ps" at the same time

"IT organizations are typically good at the run function, because that's where they spend all of their effort and money," says Kifer. "And those same organizations can be pretty good at strategy, oddly enough. It is in the implementation or execution arm of the organization where things tend to break down. You'd be surprised by how many IT organizations still don't have formal program management offices or even professional qualification certification standards for their practitioners." You may have operations down, and you've gotten your team to think strategically, but without solid execution, all of the good strategy in the world won't earn you the credibility to contribute at the strategic level. If you cannot implement, you will still fail to hurdle the Strategy versus Operations Paradox.

According to Kifer, some CIOs make the mistake of treating the three Ps (project, program, and portfolio management) as an evolution. Once they have a handle on project management, they move onto program management. And once they get good at program management, they turn their attention to the portfolio. "That's a recipe for failure," says Kifer. "In my experience, many organizations continue to view enterprise implementation and the core competencies that comprise it as an evolutionary process. They assume that the organization must progress sequentially in stair-step fashion from lowest level to highest as each is individually mastered. The reality, however, is that until the organization is managing at each of these three distinct levels simultaneously, they are at risk of failing to improve anything at all. How can you deliver a project if you don't have a sound process for determining that you are working on the right things? You don't have to be brilliant at all of it from the beginning. You need a decent working model for all three and then mature them together."

Make vendor management a core competency

With so much of its operations run by a managed service provider, one of critical competencies of the IT organization at Applied Materials had to be vendor management. "Most IT organizations go into a managed services contract with no vendor management capability whatsoever," says Kifer. "They simply do an RFP and select their vendor, only to find that they have terrible terms and conditions and that they do not have the right emphasis on cost versus performance. They are then in the position of waiting until they can get out of the contract before they can try to get it right the second time." Kifer's approach was to build a new vendor management office with experienced and certified professionals who did nothing but manage contracts and vendor relationships.

Kifer also suggests you avoid the best-in-breed model. That model, where organizations use a different vendor for nearly every function, should be a thing of the past, he says. "We've seen from experience over the last twenty years that the best-in-breed models were a nice experiment," says Kifer. "But I believe best-in-breed is one of the biggest mistakes an organization can make. The philosophy sounds good on paper, but it doesn't give you the ability to influence your vendors." Kifer and his team consolidated their vendors down to the fewest possible. "We don't believe one is appropriate, but we think that having more than three primary, strategic vendors is pushing the envelope too far."

Finally, Kifer suggests you resist the master-slave relationship with your vendors where you are so adept at squeezing them for bargain basement prices that they no longer value the relationship. "Many organizations are so focused on cost cutting that they try to grind their vendors down to the last possible penny and lose sight of the strategic nature of the relationship," says Kifer. "You have to allow your partners the opportunity to improve their margins." You can push for competitive price points, but if you squeeze them too much, you may lose an important partner.

Prove it in IT and sell it to the enterprise

"Our new model was more than just an IT solution," says Kifer. "Our program management office approach has now been extended throughout the broader organization with PMOs operating in virtually every function in the company." Likewise, Kifer's managed services model has had enterprise-wide impact, with finance, HR, and engineering all adopting the model: "We spearheaded business process management, which was lacking in the company, and that has now developed into a total quality and continuous improvement initiative that is being driven throughout the whole organization," he says. Likewise, the IT organization's M&A IT integration methodology has grown into a safe passage methodology for the entire organization to follow during an acquisition.

"New approaches to project and vendor management are some of the most difficult capabilities to introduce to companies," says Kifer. "When we started our transformation, we knew that the IT organization was not the end game. We were always trying to demonstrate results in IT and then introduce the models across the enterprise. That was our strategy."

Conclusion

There will be times during your life as a CIO that operations will rise up and demand so much of your attention that you have to tip the scales away from strategy for a while. But tip it too far and the weeds may grow around your ankles; let them grow too high and you will never cut loose. The overriding theme of this chapter is that operations management is the price of entry to the CIO position. If you cannot get a handle on your operational challenges, you will never have the opportunity to do the fun stuff. The key to solving the Operations versus Strategy Paradox is building operational excellence into your organization and getting out of the business of fighting fires. Some takeaways:

- *Get rid of the context:* If it isn't a differentiator, get it out of your house, and build a really good vendor management organization.
- *Get closer to the revenue.* Perception is often reality, and if your obstacle to strategy is the executive committee's view of IT as "all operations all the time," do something to bring in new money. Every company is becoming a technology company, which means that you have more opportunities than ever to improve your company's top line.
- *Embed IT in your corporate strategy group.* Either you or someone on your team needs to be directly involved in corporate strategy and a solid presence at those strategy meetings.
- *Don't stop with IT.* The fact is, IT organizations excel at project management, M&A methodologies, strategic planning, leadership development, and a host of other broadly applicable disciplines. How do you know when you have broken the CIO Paradox? When other business functions have adopted the models you developed in IT.

3

The Global Paradox

I remember the first time I wrote about global IT leadership, and I came across the word "glocalization." I thought to myself, when you need to invent words that sound like you are choking on a chicken bone, you probably have a paradox on your hands.

As each of you has no doubt experienced in your careers, IT leadership is hard—not impossible, but challenging to the point where you need to be incredibly talented, energetic, and committed if you are going to get it right. Add multiple countries, time zones, languages, and currencies to your purview, and your challenges only increase. A CIO's traditional approach to communication and alignment often fails under the scope and complexity of a truly global enterprise.

Before John Dick became CIO of Towers Watson, he was CIO of Western Union. Last year, Western Union moved $76 billion among 470,000 locations in more than two hundred countries and territories. "There is a distinction between being an international company and a truly global company," says Dick. "International companies tend to sell a few products or services into foreign markets through a common sales and delivery process. Western Union actually operated within and among thousands and thousands of local markets."

Prior to joining Western Union in 2008, he had roles at Crestar (now SunTrust) Bank, First Union (now Wells Fargo), GMAC, and at Regional Financial Corporation. While each of these roles certainly had its own share of challenges, Western Union was his first truly global CIO position. Given his relatively recent entry into the world of global leadership, Dick has a fresh perspective on what is probably the single most important challenge for the global CIO. "The most consistent challenge I face is achieving the right balance between global capabilities, which provide the ability to scale, and local capabilities, which provide the ability to be market or line of business responsive," he says. "You have different regulations, currencies, business practices, financial systems, and customs in different countries, and even within those countries. For us to be successful, we need to stay relevant to the customers and business opportunities at the local level."

We can read a number of paradoxes into this overarching challenge, so let's get started.

Global CIO Paradox 1: *Global Companies Tend to Export New Ideas from the Center, though Innovation Is Happening at the Edges*

Countries that are relatively new to technology innovation, and are not hobbled by thirty years of legacy-systems investment, are in the happy and productive position of leveraging the now relatively low expense of technology. With green fields all around them, they are busy innovating in ways that U.S. technology organizations cannot. So, how do you create a two-way innovation flow?

Lose your U.S.-centric mind-set

There is tremendous opportunity for global CIOs to tap into global hot spots of innovation; they just need to get out of their own way. "In the U.S., we tend to have a headstrong attitude about the way we do things, and that can be a barrier to our recognizing and leveraging the diversity of thought that exists in the world," says Dick. "As we become a more connected planet, we need a different mental framework, where we recognize that listening to ideas coming out of emerging markets will allow us to meet the needs of those markets and potentially in others. This is innovation from the edge."

Dick cites Argentina as an example. Because Argentina is a cash-based economy, consumers stand in line at Western Union locations and pay their bills in cash. This is significantly different from the practice in countries where consumers are used to paying with credit cards or online banking. "So, in Argentina, Western Union developed a system that scans the bills' barcodes and immediately processes those payments to the billers," Dick says. "The transaction time was reduced from minutes to seconds but the system also conformed to cash consumer practices in the market."

Recognizing that this innovation, born out of necessity in one country, would be effective in others, Western Union sought to deploy the new system in other countries. "The system that was developed in Argentina was rolled out in other markets with cash economies but no bar coding ability," he says.

Make succession planning global

You know the old saying, "Out of sight, out of mind"? With the centralized IT leadership team right under your nose at U.S. headquarters, it is natural for you to think first of those executives when developing your succession plan. When Dick first arrived at Western Union, he found that his leadership team was spread out across the United States and Europe. He decided that, since the company was being managed largely from its headquarters in Denver, the functional heads of IT should be co-located with the business leadership there. "However, before I left Western Union, I was reversing that direction by putting more technology leadership out into the regions and elevating those positions," says Dick. "That way, we would have more growth opportunity within the regional teams and a more diverse senior team."

Global CIO Paradox 2: *Good IT Is About Serving Your Customers, but Your Customers Can Be Radically Different from Market to Market (or the Global versus Local Paradox)*

The other day, I ordered a pair of shoes from Zappos. As a registered VIP customer (I do love my shoes), I was exasperated when the system took more than thirty seconds to process my payment. The delay was probably my own Internet connection, but I didn't care. I was annoyed! We Americans tend to want what we want when we want it; our sense of urgency is quite high, even when ordering a pair of shoes. "Consumer expectations are different from country to country," says John Dick. "In some countries, like India or the Philippines, it is the norm to spend forty-five minutes in line to conduct a transaction. And in other markets, like Brazil or France, customers will leave if they have to wait more than twenty seconds."

It is a mistake to assume that the systems that have worked for the United States will work around the globe. "CIOs who are new to a global role sometimes believe that the system capabilities that they are most used to are the best and will meet business needs throughout the world," says Dick. "And maybe for a short period of time, that's appropriate. But for sustainability, you have to understand what works in local markets and segments, and you have to build increasingly more relevant capabilities. Global companies would love to have a global payroll system, but guess what: the way that people are paid in Malaysia may not work easily with your ERP solution, so it may be more effective to leverage a local payroll processor in that country. A global CIO has to be adaptable."

Get your IT people close to the markets

It is impossible for a global CIO to understand the often subtle cultural distinctions in the buying behavior of customers around the world, so your organizational structure is incredibly important. Western Union employs agents all over the world, so local market knowledge is built right into the company's business model. Still, it was critical for Dick to structure his organization so that IT was close to those agents and was building systems based on their local market knowledge.

When Dick first arrived at Western Union, IT had a fairly decentralized structure. "We had development teams all over the world working on applications that did not adhere to common standards or architecture," he says. "So I spent the first couple of years consolidating and centralizing those functions. Once we had more structure and control around the major IT functions, my objective was to distribute IT back out to the local market again."

Global Paradox 3: *As Your Need to Communicate Increases, Your Ability to Communicate Decreases*

Ramón Baez is a CIO of Kimberly-Clark. Posting nearly $21 billion in global net sales in 2011, the company is the sixteenth largest global consumer goods company, and growing. With the company's global brands sold in more than 175 countries, having access to timely, mission-critical data is key, and Baez has IT leaders "across every boundary around the planet." Roughly half of Kimberly-Clark's 950-person IT organization, all of which reports up to Baez, is outside of the United States. Kimberly-Clark is not Baez's first time at the global rodeo. Prior to joining the company, he served as CIO for Thermo Fisher Scientific and for Honeywell International Automation and Control Solutions group. For Baez, the greatest challenge to running a global IT organization is finding a way to communicate and "be a presence" when face to face interaction is so hard to achieve.

Choose the vehicle that works for you

"The hardest part of running a global IT organization is communicating a message that everyone can understand," says Baez. "How do I make sure everyone is getting the same message?" In planning his global communication strategy, Baez thought about emulating Kimberly-Clark's CEO, who writes a weekly blog that gets thirty thousand hits a month. "I tried to do a written blog, but everyone wanted to edit it, and it didn't sound like me," he says. "It sounded like corporate speak."

So Baez chose to do a video blog instead. He sits down with his chief of staff, his communications director, and the manager of Kimberly-Clark's online IT community, and together they brainstorm enough ideas to produce twelve video spots to be aired over the next six months. Using a flip camera that sits on a little tripod, the team tapes the video and posts it on CIO Connect, the IT organization's intranet. "Last Thanksgiving, I did a video on the importance of 360-degree feedback, and called it 'Feedback Is a Gift,'" says Baez. "We had more people watch and discuss that blog than any other. It was unbelievable." Soon after Baez released the Thanksgiving post, one of his deputies started giving more frequent feedback to his team, which he had previously been reluctant to do. "I was shocked," says Baez. "I mean, this was so cool. This guy wrote this incredible feedback to one of the people who works for him because of that video."

Get personal

Whether you write a blog or do a video or express your vision through interpretive dance, the point is this: you need to be a presence in the lives of the people who work for you, especially if those people are distributed across a global landscape. And you need to let them get to know you. "You don't want to just talk about business in these blogs," says Baez. "You've got make sure that there is some personal stuff, too." Baez became a grandfather this year, so he has started to include stories about his grandson ("Moonpie") in his videos. "My year-end message this year has a snapshot of Moonpie sitting on Santa's lap and crying," says Baez. "And people talk more about that—remembering the time their child first met Santa Claus—than about our business goals."

As a result of the personal nature of his blogs, Baez's team is finding their CIO to be very approachable. "When I visit our different sites, people at all levels of the IT organization feel that they have something to talk with me about," he says.

Create a steady drumbeat

As CIO of Owens Corning, a $5.5 billion buildings materials maker, David Johns has his share of global leadership responsibilities. The company runs manufacturing facilities in thirty different countries, with a major presence in regions that include North America, Central America, South America, Europe, India, China, and Korea. Johns has a truly global IT organization, with IT leaders located in each of the company's major global regions. "You cannot say something a few times and expect everyone across your global team to understand it and start executing," says Johns. "Global communication takes a lot of work."

One of the greatest opportunities for a global organization is a follow-the-sun approach, where teams in one time zone hand off work to teams in a distant time zone, so that you wind up with an IT organization that is working on a project 24/7. "I've been trying to get a follow-the-sun process in our organization for years, but it took a while for everyone to understand that I was serious," Johns says. "They heard me say it, but they didn't really believe it for a while, and in the beginning, they were giving me more lip service than behavioral change."

Johns and his team were doing a major upgrade to the company's North American facilities, and Johns wanted the Asia Pac teams to take a significant leadership role in parts of the initiative and spend a considerable percent of their time on the project. But the Asia Pac teams were not getting on board. "Culture played a role in their resistance to leading the project," says Johns. "My IT leaders across the Asia Pac countries did not really believe they were empowered to lead a global project for the company. They believed that all of the leadership comes from our headquarters in Toledo." Johns and his CIO in Asia had to spend quite a bit of time convincing the Asia Pac IT teams that they were playing a lead on this initiative.

How do you deal with cultural expectations that are at first stronger than your organizational design plans? "There is no magic about it," says Johns. "You have to be persistent and create a cadence and a drumbeat. After a point, people either leave or they jump on board."

Global Paradox 4: *You Need to Be In-Person with Your Global Team, but You Don't Have the Time*

Ramón Baez and his communications team at Kimberly-Clark had solved the challenge of using video to communicate a clear message to the team, but they had not yet figured out how Baez could spend more interactive time with his global team and allow them to ask him questions. "I went to Shanghai, Korea, Bangkok, Sydney, and Hong Kong in August, and that was the first time in two and a half years. The trip was far overdue," he says. "How do I spend time with my teams there and in Europe and Russia without killing myself?"

Two years ago, Baez was in the United Kingdom and ran a town hall meeting for his IT organization there. "I didn't do a bunch of Power-Points or anything," he says. "I said, 'Hey, why don't you guys just ask me any questions you want? See if you can stump the CIO.'" The team asked brilliant questions, "because, you know, they're in Europe. They ask brilliant questions. That's the way they are," says Baez. He received incredibly positive feedback about the town hall, and the team asked him to supplement his in-person meetings with video conferences in a similar style to the town hall he had just led. "I said, 'Really? That would be good enough for you?'" says Baez. "So we gave it a try."

For the first few video town halls, Baez asked that questions be submitted in advance, and then he took time to work with his team to put together a response. "That didn't go over real well," he says. "They wanted a more direct, immediate interaction." So, for the next quarterly teleconference, Baez just walked in having done no preparation. "They asked me really hard questions; it was great, " he says. The session went so well that Baez has now done eight quarterly video sessions with the U.K. group. "I have not been there in two years," he says. "And to them, it feels like I am there all the time."

After the success of the U.K. video venture, Baez decided to try the same approach with Asia Pac. "With Asia Pac, we tried the pre-submitted questions format again, and it still didn't work," he says. So for the next town hall, Baez asked the team to send questions via instant message to a facilitator in Australia, and that person asked Baez the question. "In China, their English is getting so good that they often just asked me the questions directly. When I was in Bangkok, we did a video town hall for the whole region. I was amazed by how many questions I was asked."

Baez has now baked these virtual town halls into his calendar; he runs them quarterly in Europe and three times a year in Asia and Latin America.

Baez has some advice for global CIOs who would like actually to sleep in their own beds at night and who see virtual town halls as a viable means toward that end: "Don't preach or present to them. Just let them ask you questions. That's what they really want to do." Baez also suggests that you invite one of your key regional IT leaders to run the meetings with you. "With Latin America and Asia Pac, we are growing so fast and there is so much going on there, I absolutely need to have one or two of my deputies with me. I will answer questions more broadly, but they can get into more of the specifics," he says.

Global Paradox 5: *Local Ties Can Be Stronger than Global Allegiances*

Don Goldstein had been CIO of Trammell Crow Company, which was acquired by CBRE, a large commercial real estate services company, in 2005. When he joined the larger company, it had four CIOs, each heading a major global region. In 2009, the executive leadership at CBRE decided to establish a more globalized structure, with global platforms for some of the company's major processes. Goldstein was made global CIO.

"Just by saying that we are moving to a global strategy doesn't make it so," says Goldstein. "You can lull yourself into a false sense of security by assuming that if the CEO says 'global' and makes you the global CIO that all of the sudden, you can build a global organization." The ties between country managers and their IT leaders can be very strong, based on a shared culture and years of working together. While some regional IT and business leaders will see the value of a globalized, centralized IT organization, others will smile and nod and do very little to get on board. "You have to be careful that you are not just taking the IT structure that is embedded in those regions and assuming that they will focus their efforts on global initiatives. Some regional leaders will acknowledge that they report to you on paper, but in their minds, they still report to their country presidents. That's who they see every day," says Goldstein. "Even when the leadership buys in to the global strategy, you need to make sure that you continue to support the regions as you move to a global organization."

Global Paradox 6: *You Need to Act Fast, but Creating a Global Structure Takes Time*

Building a global organization can take years. "If you are a CIO with a short tenure, the sand may run out of the hourglass before you are done," says Goldstein. "This is the time to develop patience as a leader. Especially when you are dealing with resistance that comes out of your regional businesses, you may need to let things work themselves out over time." When you are moving from a regional organization to a global one, expectations management really comes into play. You may have a global president asking why the IT organization isn't fully globalized yet; you are the CIO, just go in there and take control! "The global business leaders may be seeing all of the country presidents nodding their heads in agreement about the global strategy, when in reality, there are countervailing forces within the regions that favor the status quo," says Goldstein. "The trick is to act quickly when the IT and business leaders are truly on board, and in the meantime, help the global leaders to understand the virtue of patience."

Conclusion

Running a truly global IT organization is one of the most formidable leadership challenges of all time. Distance, time zones, and differing cultural norms create awe-inspiring obstacles to communication and relationship building. And the "what processes do I globalize and what do I keep local?" question requires constant attention. It is no wonder that the job of the global CIO is rife with so many paradoxes. Yet, CIOs are breaking these paradoxes all the time, through a number of approaches:

- *Develop a global communications plan:* Use video, tell stories, hire communications specialists, make it constant, and don't ever assume that just because you said it three times, they've heard it in every corner of the globe.

- *Tap into global innovation.* Your teams on the fringes are free to think out of the legacy box, when your U.S. organization often is not. Create a global innovation flow by challenging assumptions that "invented here" is best.
- *Be patient:* Change takes time, and even more so in a global basis. If you push too quickly, you will wind up with resentment and entrenchment and a fractured organization that never realizes the potential of a truly global enterprise.

PART II

Your Stakeholders: Will the Business Ever Love IT?

4

The Futurist versus Archivist Paradox

The other day, I was on the phone with the CIO of a company that had acquired some fairly sizable businesses over the past five years. The lion's share of this CIO's IT strategy was to integrate these companies. "But then, like a tsunami," she said, "from every fissure and pore of our employee and customer base there arose a wave of new technology demands, and I don't have the budget."

What she is talking about, of course, are consumer technologies. The business has always had an insatiable appetite for IT, and as CIO, you have always had to manage what must be the ultimate CIO Paradox, supply versus demand. But with consumer technologies, the situation has grown more acute. Before the consumerization of IT, the demand for new technologies might have come from the head of sales who needed a better way to manage customer data, or from the head of HR who was looking for a better payroll system. Now, everybody and his brother are clamoring for a piece of the IT budget. The CEO wants to use her iPad at work, the new field sales group wants to access the CRM system on the road, and your administrative assistant wants corporate e-mail on her iPhone.

You've spent the last ten years of your career trying to convince your company of the value of IT. Well, guess what? Everybody gets it! They all understand how important technology is to their jobs. Congratulations. Your job must be much easier now. If it isn't, then you've stumbled upon an brand new CIO Paradox: *The business is getting smarter about technology, but your job is getting harder.*

The tendency for employees to drive technology spending is not new, of course. No matter the leadership skills and visionary brilliance of the CIO, IT has always been in the position of responding to employee-driven IT investment, just as it should be. "Thirty years ago, users started bringing PCs into work and sort of undermining the corporate IT function, which had been running mainframes in the data center," says Ralph Loura, CIO of the Clorox Company. "And corporate IT cried out 'We can't control that hardware! Those PCs are not secure!' But we figured it out, and we caught up. Then ten years ago, RIM shipped its first device, a two-way texter, which users brought into the enterprise, and again IT resisted the new technology because we couldn't manage or control it, but we made it work."

For decades, employees have pushed the envelope of IT standards with their technology demands. "The difference now is the pace at which it is happening," says Loura. In the past, users introduced new technologies to the company, but those technologies wouldn't really explode until the enterprise adopted them. "Enterprise adoption gave new technologies their heft, their volume, and their ubiquity, and then they would bleed back into the consumer space."

Now, the opposite is happening. "The first place a device or a new multi-platform file sharing service shows up is in the consumer space," says Loura. "Then, after gaining scale and broad consumer adoption, those technologies come into the enterprise."

What's radically different about the last two years is that the large scale adoption of new technologies takes place outside the enterprise first; by the time consumers lay their favorite new technologies at the CIO's door, the demand for that technology is already widespread and staggering. "IT is left scrambling because the rate of enterprise adoption is not slow and steady," says Loura. "It is an overnight-demand explosion."

A few months ago, I was chatting with a CIO who told me that one Monday morning he was riding in the elevator with the president of his company's North American business. The executive turned to him and asked, "Jim, why is it that when I come to work each morning, I feel like I am stepping back in time?"

If employees can sit in their houses and set up Twitter and Google and Facebook accounts in five minutes, why does it take eighteen months, they wonder, to build the same capabilities at work? This brings us to one of the more pernicious paradoxes under the consumerization banner: *The more your employees love technology, the more they dislike IT.*

Before we move on to solutions (we'll get there, I promise!), let's bring up one more challenge wrought by technology consumerization. For this, I must tell a story: when I first got into recruiting, I was hungry for new clients and I agreed to two search engagements I really should not have taken. The searches were for positions in isolated locations that were not of interest to the technology executive population, and they were for companies unwilling to pony up the compensation necessary to attract the right talent. My clients were not particularly fast about reviewing new candidates, so when my team and I did uncover someone good, we could not lock them down; the interview and feedback phase took way too long.

After several months, my other business development efforts started to bear fruit and I began to receive calls about better search engagements. I took them on, but I still had to work the first two searches; they never went away. I got overloaded, and I couldn't deliver candidates to my new clients quickly enough. We finally got "the dogs out of the kennels," to quote my director of recruiting, Carol Lynn Thistle, and we got our delivery organization in order. But the backlog of searches nearly killed my search practice in its very first year.

That experience reminds me of the situation that CIOs find themselves in when it comes to consumer technologies. "IT used to run the big corporate data center, a centralized computing infrastructure," says Loura. "Then we moved into the client/server revolution, but we still had to run centralized computing. Then mobility erupted, which we had to figure out while still doing all of the other things we had been doing. I don't know a single large-scale IT function that doesn't still have some data center somewhere doing centralized computing. But the business expects us to put all of our focus on new technologies. Now, we are chasing this collaborative social environment, but that doesn't mean we can stop running our ERP systems. Right now, IT is being asked to do many things that are very different than what we used to do. That is making it challenging to provide the value that the business wants as quickly as it wants it without IT costs spiraling out of control."

This seems like the perfect time to bring in what I believe is one of the most fascinating CIO Paradoxes of all: as a CIO today, you need to be out in front of the business, envisioning the way your customers will use mobile technology and other emerging technologies to interact with your business three years from now. You are certainly not alone out there in front. You have sales, marketing, and other departmental executives standing alongside you. However, unlike those sales and marketing executives, you drag with you, like cement shoes, the technology decisions your company made fifteen years ago, before you even came on board. The head of sales couldn't care less how your products were sold fifteen years ago, but you cannot be so cavalier about the past. The paradox? *As CIO, you are your company's futurist and its archivist.*

Like every CIO Paradox, the paradox produced by consumerization is simply a reality. And your job, as CIO, is to figure out how to get past it. So, what do you do when the pace of technology change is so fast and so widespread that you and your legacy systems are caught in catch-up mode and the business's expectations far outweigh your ability to meet them?

Learn to Sell Legacy Improvements

I would wager that every CIO of every company faces some form of the Futurist versus Archivist paradox, and Tom Murphy, formerly CIO of $80 billion pharmaceutical company AmerisourceBergen, is one of them. "This is probably one of the core paradoxes for the CIO," says Murphy. "Whether it's about consumer technologies or ERP or e-mail, legacy begins the day you put something in. We have always had to deal with it."

In 2004, Murphy joined AmerisourceBergen and inherited a thirty-year-old mainframe environment with hundreds of master applications in a company with revenue projected to climb from $55 billion to $80 billion over the next eight years. The company's two largest competitors were moving off the mainframe, so it was clear to Murphy that the company had to make a bold move. "My CEO was saying that the road is littered with companies who have tried to do an ERP, so I knew it would be a tough sell," says Murphy.

Use visuals to make your case

Murphy realized that if he talked and talked about the value of an ERP system, he would be met with skepticism and glazed-over eyeballs, so he decided to try something visual.

First, Murphy and his team had AmerisourceBergen's business leaders rate all of the firm's applications in terms of their importance to the organization. They then mapped the applications against the last twelve months of help desk tickets and outages. With this data in hand, they developed a heat map of the eighty most critical applications, which showed that forty-five of them failed at least once a month. The map showed that, over time, there would be more and more red zones. "I was able to say to the CEO, 'Look at how this all maps up. Your executives are saying that these applications are the most important, and they will not be able to generate revenue if they are not available. Your people told me this; I'm not making it up.'"

When the company had its next serious outages in its customer order entry environment, his CEO saw the light. "When he called to ask about the outage, he said: 'Is this what you've been talking about?' That was the day we started the process of selling the board on ERP," Murphy says.

What Murphy's experience shows us is that seeing is believing. It is hard to sell concepts like ERP and infrastructure upgrades through proposals and reports. "No CEO is going to listen to you talk about the stack and the complexity of your middleware," says Murphy. "I am a huge believer in the power of maps to illustrate the reality of the technology environment," he says. "It moves the conversation from an emotional one to a fact-based one."

As another example, Murphy created a map that showed where the data resided in the current applications environment. "I put the map on the wall and asked the CEO to tell me what he wanted to know about a customer," says Murphy. "He would ask a question and then I would walk him through how that data had to travel through all of those systems to finally get to him." Once Murphy's CEO was shown the tortuous route from question to answer, he had a much deeper understanding of the challenges of the current environment.

Find your burning platform

"The burning platform is your friend if it doesn't kill you," says Murphy. "Those two outages easily could have cost me my job. In an environment where you are .08 percent net profit and you have lost your core ordering environment for weeks at time, it is easy for the company to call for someone's head."

There is almost always a burning platform in IT. If you are communicating about IT investments effectively, you can use that burning platform to make your point for you. "What saved me is that we had been having this candid dialogue about our technology environment," says Murphy. "My colleagues even told me later that the moment those outages occurred was the moment when the CEO finally crossed the Rubicon. After that, it was just a discussion of how much it will cost and how much it will hurt."

Probably the most important lesson to learn from Murphy's experience is this: If you are going to be successful in managing the Futurist versus Archivist Paradox, you need to develop the ability to sell foundational improvements to your executive leadership team. "When people are asked to make a major investment in something that doesn't feel competitive or sexy, they tend to resist," says Murphy. "The sales force and operating teams think of improvements in foundational platforms like a tax." But if you cannot sell improvements, you will never break the paradox, and you will always be burdened with legacy. You will layer complexity on top of legacy in an effort to innovate. And, as Tom Murphy puts it, "You will make the mess worse, and your company will find you out."

Get your assets out of your shop

The more you are burdened by legacy technologies, the more time you will spend managing your infrastructure and the greater the likelihood your business partners will get antsy and start making their own technology decisions. If that's fine with you, then keep things as they are. But if, as CIO, you would like to maintain a high level of involvement in your company's technology investments, you will need to get some infrastructure off your plate. "What I see happening is that CIOs in many companies are losing control over technology in their companies," says Tom Murphy. "The really cool new stuff is not happening through the IT organization, it is happening everywhere else. The CIOs who can focus on what's new will be relevant, but the CIOs who continue to focus on enterprise systems will be replaced. Our job is to get as much iron and heavy assets out of our facilities so that we can quickly move to the new platform paradigm."

One approach that Murphy suggests is to create a small group of your most creative thinkers and have them examine your data centers and set a plan for reducing your assets, while you leave your infrastructure people in place. "Don't turn your infrastructure people into change agents," he says.

Focus on Architecture

The age of consumerization has brought with it a paradigm shift in the way organizations select and implement new technologies, and many CIOs are making dramatic changes in how they think about their architecture. It is interesting to note, by the way, that there is no other organization that undergoes paradigm shifts quite so frequently as IT. Certainly not finance; basic accounting rules have been around for what, a thousand years? As Geir Ramleth, CIO of Bechtel, puts it, "You look at human resources, marketing, or sales and operations. They are all relatively mature and the overall rate of change is very low. Look at finance and accounting: double-sided accounting started in Venice in the fifteenth century." IT is like a teenager living with his grandparents. He is changing every day, and they don't understand him.

"For the last fifteen years, the IT organization has been focused on integration," says Clorox's Ralph Loura. "Our paramount role has been to integrate big on-premise software solutions and large business intelligence platforms. Even our analytics work has really been about data integration." In the integration paradigm, you control all of the pieces in between the systems you are integrating. "In this scenario, I have SOA-level control," says Loura. "I can control what fields are exposed in each step to ensure that the data is properly formatted to work correctly in the next step." With consumerization and cloud services, the role of IT moves from integrator to orchestrator, and orchestration is different because you no longer have direct control of all of the pieces. You may use one third-party solution for one process and another for a different process, as you build, for example, an end-to-end work flow for employees from onboarding through retirement. "But how do you do that when you don't own everything in the middle?" asks Loura. "You do that through very rigorous architectural thinking, planning, and review. You need to ensure that you have very clear APIs and boundary sets so you can guarantee that service will work end to end, even though you don't control what's inside the box at each step."

There are a number of technical approaches to managing IT's new role as orchestrator, but the overall point I would like to highlight from Loura's comments goes beyond a specific technology: the IT organization's ability to deliver in this new cloud based, consumer-based computing environment relies on its having a disciplined architecture. "Architecture is a belief system," says Loura. "Architecture is defining what you truly believe in: Do you believe in everything as a service? Do you believe in locking down your PCs? Every business is different and has different needs, which will impact IT's belief system. And then governance is having the discipline to put that belief system into action." If you have an architectural belief system that your business partners, your staff, and your vendors all adopt as gospel, you will be able orchestrate what amounts to a new IT delivery supply chain, and you may even keep up with the onslaught of business demands coming your way.

Just Do It

Nowhere is the Futurist versus Archivist Paradox as acute as in the health-care industry, where legacy infrastructure is spread out among a huge, disorganized, disconnected array of organizations. "Whether you are a payer or a provider, you rely on data, and that data engine is either a transaction system or an electronic medical record system," says Scott Blanchette, CIO of Vanguard Health Systems, a $5 billion health-care provider. "These systems have become huge, unwieldy, ineffective beasts that make hospitals more expensive and less efficient. Patient data has become digitized but not integrated, so we are creating a stovepipe situation that is actually more dangerous than when we were all on paper a generation ago. We are a highly fractured industry vertical."

This CIO Paradox as it affects health care is particularly vexing because it is so extreme: the legacy side of the equation is a total mess and the futurist side—the possibility of an integrated health-care ecosystem—could be life-changing. "The health-care industry would benefit tremendously from big data analytics," says Blanchette. "If we can do what has never been done and correlate data about a person over the course of his lifetime, and put that single source of truth together with mobility, that's when the magic happens." With the marriage of mobility and predictive health analytics, your health-care provider would not only be aware that you are at medical risk, she could help you prevent negative outcomes. "Your doctor can say, 'Martha, you're going to have a heart attack in a year, so I'm giving you a virtual coach and an online support network that will help you manage your health," says Blanchette. "No one likes to deal with the health-care system, because it's awful. (I don't like to, and I work in the industry.) But if we can make dealing with health care 'iPad simple,' we can actually improve people's lives."

So, on the one hand we have the dream of an integrated health-care infrastructure that allows consumers and providers one source of truth, and on the other we have the reality of a fragmented health-care system with no clear path toward integration. How do you innovate on a broken platform? "I didn't put in the legacy system, and I don't feel compelled to preserve it," says Blanchette. "I'm not here to fight the old fights and solve the old problems. George Patton circumnavigated the Nazis in France and just marched on to Berlin. He knew that it would be foolish to fight in France when he was going to win eventually, anyway."

Blanchette and his team at Vanguard Health Systems follow a set of principles when developing new technology strategies and products to provide health care to consumers.

1. *No more incumbents.* "If your technology comes out of a box, we won't buy it," says Blanchette. "We are religiously committed to not working with traditional technology solution providers. All enterprise software providers have the same fundamental flaws: poor quality, a lack of innovation, and no incentive to change. In the health-care industry, the top five enterprise software providers own 67 percent of our space. If you are an incumbent in this space, you have benefited from our chaos, and you are not my most trusted business partner."

2. *Find the entrepreneurs.* "There is a reason for the success of salesforce. com," says Blanchette. "It is a portable solution that is hosted in the cloud. Our goal is to give our patients and providers an experience like Facebook and other social media. We have a very strong predisposition to working with entrepreneurs who can bring the advancements they've made in other industries to health care."

3. *Let the data stay put.* "Our preference is to work with partners who resist the urge to put all of the data in a gigantic data warehouse. That's an old way of thinking. Index the data where it is."

4. *Know the data analytics provider marketplace.* "We are exploring the analytics space to partner with firms that have the capability to provide us with insights we have never had before. Getting to the data is one thing, but making sense of it is another."

5. *Get rid of legacy devices.* In 2011, smartphones and tablets outsold PCs and laptops for the first time. "This was a momentous event that Spielberg should be making movies about," says Blanchette. "For forty years, PCs have dominated, and they lost last year. The Rubicon has been crossed, and we are never going back. Why in the world would you force people to do something at work that is so wildly different from what they do at home? You will only be met with resistance."

In Blanchette's first year as CIO of Vanguard, he attended a leadership meeting with five hundred people. "Almost all of them had two devices: one we were paying for and one they actually liked," he says. "When I thought about the massive duplication of expense and work flow processes, I decided to get rid of every corporate-sponsored cell phone. We subsidize the device, but because it is our employee's lifestyle, we let it be our employee's choice." Like cell phones, PCs are going away, and Apple and Google will dominate the next wave of computing. "If we can't play to where the puck is going, let's at least play to where it's at," says Blanchette. "Don't feel obliged to solve old, unsolvable problems. Start down a new path."

Tighten Your Connection to the Business

We are at a particularly interesting moment in time, when IT is embedded in everything we do, from running the business to developing new products to bringing those products to market. We are also at a moment in time when it is easier than ever for business executives to wave their credit cards at software-as-a-service providers and download their own technology. This takes the "shadow IT" problem, which has amounted to a mere nuisance for CIOs in the past, to a whole new level. And it leads us to another CIO Paradox: *You are accountable for IT performance, security, and support costs, but IT vendors often go around you to sell to your business peers.*

Now, I must admit that when I have brought this particular paradox up at CIO conferences, I get some serious pushback. "We *want* our business partners to innovate with technology," CIOs tell me. "What's *wrong* with the business making technology investment decisions?" My response is, "There is absolutely nothing wrong with your business partners investing directly in technology, as long as you are agreed on what those investments are, how they will be secured, integrated, and paid for, and, of course, what the return on those investments is expected to be."

Boeing, not surprisingly, is filled with people who know a few things about engineering and technology. "As a result, there is this huge tendency for people across the company to do their own thing when it comes to technology," says Kim Hammonds, CIO. "And over the years, the lines have blurred in terms of what counts as engineering and what counts as IT."

Hammonds considers it a core part of her job to insert herself in the engineering organizations to be sure they are conforming to standards. "It's a balancing act that we walk every day," she says. "We cannot stop the engineers from making technology decisions, but we need to get in there to make sure the IT content is protected, secure, and efficient. We'll ask them, 'Do you really need to be running that lab equipment yourself?' When you have people who are constantly trying to build things and attach them to the network, you need to find ways to manage them or costs will get out of control."

Let the data set you free

Hammonds' approach to keeping engineers from building and running their own technology is to let her data do the talking. "If you can use data to demonstrate that the organization is more secure and cost effective when IT is involved in technology decisions, you will win the argument," she says. "You let the data set you free. If you have the facts, you take the emotion and hypotheses out of the conversation. But it's a conversation we are having all the time. It's never really over."

This brings us to another skill that CIOs who have broken the paradox use all the time, but before I mention it, I must tell a little story. The other day, I couldn't connect to my wireless network. I had a busy, busy day ahead, with chapters to write, proposals to submit, and candidate résumés to review. I needed my connection! As I sat there trying this and that, I found myself becoming more and more angry until I was overcome with rage, a white hot rage targeted directly at Mike, who provides my firm with IT support. Was I irrational? Certainly! Was I unfair? Of course! Did I care? Not at all. When it comes to technology, we want what we want when we want it, and we often act like toddlers when we don't get it, particularly when our company is losing money because of a technology problem that we don't understand (and cannot control).

Thus, a critical skill for breaking the paradox is the ability to use data to diffuse the situation. Tom Murphy used maps to build a case for ERP, and Hammonds uses metrics on security and costs to maintain control of IT in a culture of engineers. When you are faced with a system outage and a frustrated executive, the sooner you can get to the facts the sooner you can move past the conflict and toward a solution.

Install a client management function

When it comes to tightening your connections to the business, you need to think hard about the people you have stationed at those critical intersections. Most IT organizations have a point person for the business, someone they can hold accountable for IT delivery for that function or business and who translates business requirements back to the IT organization. At Clorox, Ralph Loura has defined this role as *client manager.* "Our client managers are expected to build an account plan for a business group, sort of like a sales executive. A client manager will sit down with the products supply manager to ensure we are aligned on his priorities."

Once the client manager has defined the road map, she sits down with the solution designer, that rare professional with a beautifully blended skill set of technology and business knowledge. "The solution designer role is very important; we are attempting to grow it internally at Clorox because it's a really unique skill set," says Loura. "This is someone who knows a specific set of business processes and has broad enough technology knowledge to figure out how to orchestrate a solution to solve a particular business need in a way that is tightly aligned to our IT architecture and governance."

These people do not fall out of trees. In fact, the solution designer, like the enterprise architect, is a perfect embodiment of the CIO Paradox. If this person is at a manager level, he is likely to be somewhat of a technical specialist, because IT people still grow up in silos. But he needs to be a specialist in a specific set of business processes *and* have a broad enough view of technology that he can be open minded when it comes to solutions. "You might be able to find a solution designer who knows product supply and ERP," says Loura. "But they are not familiar with the newest Internet tool. They tend to find the solution in what they know, which may not necessarily be the best solution."

So, where do you find these rare birds? Many CIOs import talent from the business, which may work for the client manager role but not for the solution designer position. "You cannot get solution designers from the business, because business people know the process but they don't often think in IT terms," says Loura. "And if you don't think in IT, you don't think systems and structures. You can learn how to translate, but you'll never be fluent. Our solution designers need to be fluent."

Loura looks to former consultants for candidates. "Someone who has spent the last ten years of his life consulting in, say, the supply chain space has seen every problem, every business model, every business process, and every mix of technology at one point or another," he says. "They've got this breadth of technology experience, and they understand how to craft IT solutions."

Of course, there are assimilation risks when hiring a consultant. "Consultants don't always make the best employees," Loura notes. "People who have been consulting for too long can have trouble adjusting to corporate life, and they don't always understand the downstream impact of the choices they make. So, we spend a lot of time in our interviews digging into those two areas."

Loura also rotates his client managers into application support and maintenance for a year, "so that they live with the choices they have made as client managers." His hope is that they come out with a deeper understanding of the technology solutions they are managing.

The good news for all of you up-and-comers out there is that by the time you are CIO, your predecessors, like Loura, will have been working hard to develop this paradox-breaking group of blended professionals. And since my husband tells me that I am not retiring until I am seventy-five, that's good news for me, too.

Conclusion

For a small percentage of CIOs, the era of consumerization and mobility has made IT delivery faster and easier. But for most, it has caused an increase in business demand that has the potential to overwhelm. As Daniel Priest, CIO of Toyota Financial Services, put it, "Our sales and marketing teams' heads are swimming with ideas about how to accommodate the digital consumer, but we're living on a legacy servicing system. Their ability to imagine what's possible far outstrips our ability to accommodate them."[3]

Priest is hardly alone. The majority of CIOs I speak to tell me that their number one challenge is running new things on old iron. This particular paradox is so big, so complex, and so entrenched, that it will take more than a book, and certainly more than a chapter, to tackle it. Still, there are actions you can take:

- *Manage the intersections with the business.* It is easier than ever for your business peers to buy their own technology. The tighter your connection points to your company's most important business leaders, the more integrated and efficient your infrastructure. The people who straddle the business and IT will determine your success. Do you have the right people in those roles?
- *Revisit old assumptions.* When was the last time you took a close look at your architecture? Does your "belief system" hold up in the current environment? Have you assessed your vendors in our new world of software as a service? Are your traditional vendors the right partners for the future? We are right in the middle of a major technology paradigm shift, one that is greater—I would wager—

than the digital revolution of the late 90s. While some of your traditional approaches to architecture and vendor selection may hold up, others may need to change.

- *Make a compelling case for legacy improvements:* Whether you use maps, data or burning platforms, you need to be able to sell the unsexy side of IT. This has always been a challenge for CIOs, but with your business peers hungry for apps, products, and devices, the skill is a must-have.

5

The "IT *and* the Business" Paradox

I have spent an inordinate amount of time thinking about the word "and."
You would expect the word to function as a connector, to imply the
togetherness of two entities, like "mom and pop" or "spaghetti and meat-
balls." Yet the phrase "IT and the business," which I continue to hear all
the time, despite CIOs' claims that they have done away with it, does
not work that way at all. Rather, the "and" in "IT and the business" con-
notes separateness and difference, an "us and them" perception that has
plagued IT organizations since the beginning of their existence.

We don't say, "finance and the business" or "sales and the business"
or even "HR and the business." Why is it that IT alone is treated like
an outsider? If we get out our history books and look at what traditionally causes one group to push another to the margins, we typically find a
healthy dose of fear and ignorance. Clearly, there is something about IT
that causes uncertainty and confusion among members of the executive
committee. CEOs, who have typically done stints in finance, sales, and
operations, have never run IT and they do not understand the function,
its tools, its staff, or, most importantly, where all that money goes. This

lack of understanding makes CEOs fairly uncomfortable with IT, and predisposes them to separate themselves from it. Hence the paradox: *You are intimately involved in every fact of the business, yet you are often considered separate and removed from it.*

"We may have a seat at the table, but we have not gotten as close to the table as heads of HR and finance," says Colleen Wolf, CIO of Ventura Foods, reflecting back on her IT past CIO experiences. "Salespeople understand finance, and finance people understand HR, but no one fully understands what IT actually does. So we are on an island." Will the scenario change when our current generation of business executives retires and makes way for a new generation of more technically savvy leaders? "In many ways, consumerization is making the situation worse," says Wolf. "Everyone understands what it takes to download an app, so they think IT is easy. When in reality, IT is just getting more complicated."

But the culpability does not rest solely with business leaders. There are still a decent number of CIOs—and I meet them every day—who exacerbate the "us and them" divide. As an executive recruiter, I am often hired by companies to find a replacement for the sitting CIO because he is not working out. Usually, there is some pressing reason, like a global single-instance ERP program run amok, but that is merely the proverbial straw that broke the CEO's back. When I interview this frustrated CEO, she will describe a scene where all of the executives are sitting at one end of the table discussing corporate goals with a shared understanding of how their business works. And far at the other end of the table sits the CIO, with a propeller on his head, spewing SOA and cloud and banging away on his iPhone. While I am being slightly hyperbolic to make a point, the situation I describe comes quite close to reality. I cannot tell you how many times I have been asked to replace a CIO who cannot build relationships with his executive peers and cannot inspire trust in the IT organization. *It happens all the time.*

Why? Why are we still dealing with this issue? How many articles has *CIO* magazine published about speaking the language of the business, building relationships with business leaders, being a business leader first and a technologist second? While a huge group of CIOs get it and are bona fide business leaders, another huge group does not.

Doug Myers, CIO of Pepco Holdings, Inc. (PHI), a regional energy holding company that provides utility services to nearly two million customers, has his own theory about this chasm between the business and IT. "Think about it. IT people have a different language, we have specialized training, our job descriptions don't resemble business job descriptions, and neither do our titles," he says. "And because our skills are transferable from one industry to another, we can fall into the trap of thinking of ourselves as IT professionals, as opposed to industry professionals. In many ways, the gap between the business and IT is natural, and to reduce it, we need to battle the natural order of things."

Battling the natural order of things is akin to rolling a boulder uphill. But battling the natural order of things—including trepidation about the unknown, an innate distrust of technology, and a desire to keep things as they are—is probably the most constant part of the CIO's job. So, let's get started.

Revisit Some Communication Basics

For every CIO who bows to the natural order of things, by walking and talking technology and separating herself from the business, there are many who do not. These CIOs tell me that the concept of "IT and the business" drives them up the wall, and that through a number of changes, both semantic and operational, they have removed the separation between IT and the business and now live together as one. In other words, when it comes to the divide between IT and the business, they have broken the paradox.

Leslie Jones is CIO for Motorola Solutions, Inc., the $9 billion provider of mission critical communication systems and services for government and retail enterprises. Jones joined Motorola in 2000 with the acquisition of General Instrument, where she served as CIO. Since joining Motorola, Jones has served as the vice president for IT for Motorola's enterprise mobility solutions and home and networks mobility businesses, and as deputy CIO for Motorola.

When Jones joined General Instrument as CIO, she walked into an organization where the CEO viewed IT as one of the company's biggest problems. Senior management spent a great deal of time lamenting the IT organization's performance, management, and direction. As the new CIO, it was Jones' job to fix the problem.

Downsize your standard reports

Before Leslie Jones became CIO, her predecessor had produced a weekly report for the executive committee, as did every functional leader in the company. The IT reports were eight-page descriptions of what had happened that week and contained an infinite amount of technical detail about what was going on in IT. "Nobody cared," says Jones. "So I cancelled those reports and put out a one-pager that clearly stated what got done that week. It was very simple—and very short."

Immediately after sending out the one-pager, Jones received a note from the CEO saying that hers was the best IT weekly report he had ever seen. "All I did was extract the most important information from the pages and pages of techno-talk," said Jones. "I only told the business what they needed to hear."

This seems pretty straightforward. Just tell the business what they need to know. And yet I continue to hear from CEOs that their CIOs cannot deliver a presentation without technical acronyms. Why do so many CIOs have this need to use rich technical detail in their communication?

As a recruiter, I have interviewed a tremendous number of CIOs, and I can assess communication skills in the first ten minutes. I ask candidates to tell me about a recent accomplishment, and they typically answer in one of two ways. Either they talk about organizational transformation or business goals or new revenue, or they take me, step by step, through the details of their technology portfolio. Happily, there are more candidates in the first group than in the second, but the second is still sizeable.

Part of the problem may stem from the fact that IT is difficult, and not everyone can manage it. And IT is underappreciated. One of the CIO Paradoxes that resonates most with CIO audiences is "*Your many successes are invisible; your few mistakes are highly visible.*" Or as Geir Ramleth, CIO of Bechtel, puts it, "Being a CIO is like being a goalie. No one knows your name until you let one in." Many CIOs believe: "You only think about me and my team when something goes wrong, but we are working really hard all the time, and I need you to understand that." Hence the pages and pages of technical detail that CIOs put in their reports.

I can relate. When my recruiting team and I are having a tough time finding that elusive perfect candidate, one who has the right blend of technical and business skills, is a good cultural fit, is in the right location, and comes at the right price, we want to show our clients the hundreds of people we have reached out to, the fifty people we've rejected, and all the work we are doing on the client's behalf. But all they really want to know is, "Where are my candidates?"

Like many CIOs, Jones has gotten over the need to "show her work." "I'm not interested in discussing how hard it was. I'm not interested in discussing where we are on things. I'm not interested in discussing how we did it, because from a business's point of view, that is uninteresting," she says. "The only thing worth discussing is the result you produce for the business."

Consider the negative implications of IT-only meetings

During the early part of Jones' CIO tenure she learned that, historically, the CIO held a town hall with the whole IT organization to go over quarterly results. "I'm thinking, this is nearly the stupidest thing

I've ever seen. We are the business, so we belong in the business's town hall," says Jones. "The IT-only meetings were set up to make IT feel good about itself, but you can't make IT feel good about itself if it's not deeply entrenched as a valued member of the business."

Revamp your awards programs

When Mike Capone became CIO of ADP in 2008, the $10 billion global business process outsourcing company had an employee achievement award; the CEO would stand up in front of thousands of employees and recognize one of them for a significant contribution. "People in the IT group would always nominate each other, and it was typically, 'This guy stayed up all night for weeks and solved this brutal technology problem,'" says Capone. "But there was no tie back to the business. The guy who was nominated had worked all night to fix a problem that nobody seemed to care about." Capone changed the nominating process so that a business line leader would nominate an IT person and talk about the impact the nominee had on business transformation." While Capone also changed his organization's objectives and bonus plans to align with business objectives, the point here is that he changed something symbolic. Symbolic gestures like nominations and awards can have a significant impact on bringing IT together with the business. Don't overlook them.

Live and die by your communications calendar

According to many of the CIOs I have spoken to, one of the best investments they have made is in a communications specialist. When Heather Campbell was CIO of Canadian Pacific Railway, she and her communications manager worked with a company called ThinkUp Communications to do a comprehensive stakeholder analysis: Who would Campbell need to communicate with across the company, about what, how often, and through what channels? "We then built a rolling calendar and I stuck to it faithfully," says Campbell. The calendar included "lunch & learns," team meetings, "VP drop-ins," community forums (which Campbell substituted for town halls, a term she feels is overused), quarterly and annual reports, and even "traction e-cards," which notify winners of the company-wide employee excellence award program. On that note, Campbell also created a special CIO Gold Traction award for "Living the Values." "At my community forums, I made a point of awarding one or two of these for people who just did a good job day in and day out. It was my way of keeping the values of the 'new IT' front and center."

Canadian Pacific Railway employees were particularly responsive to Campbell's twenty-four-page high-gloss IT Year in Review. "People saw that the most successful IT projects were being highlighted in this glossy showcase, and they wanted to be in there," says Campbell. "When I handed out the report, everyone rifled through it to see if they could find their picture. One of our business partners said 'The grain order entry project made the front of the book!' She was proud to be a part of that project."

Recognize the Innate Power of Language

The pen is mightier than the sword, and the fate of nations has been altered by a well-written manifesto. Political movements have been launched by a single, passionate speech, and marketing departments spend millions of dollars coming up with the perfect three words to describe their products. Language matters, and it is one of your most powerful tools in bringing IT together with the business.

Get rid of the jargon, once and for all

Doug Myers, CIO of Pepco Holdings, served in a variety of non-IT leadership roles before moving into IT. For Jones and Myers, business language is his native tongue, and he can turn all of his attention to teaching his teams to be bilingual. "For me, learning the language of the business was not much of a personal challenge, because I do not have a technical background," says Myers. "And because of that, I had never acquired any specialized technical training or been immersed in the language of technology."

For Myers, who grew up in the business, adopting the language of the business is natural. "But a CIO with a technical background needs to unlearn, or at a minimum, rely less upon what got him there in the first place," says Myers. "That's the personal, most internal aspect of fighting the natural order of things."

For Myers, getting his organization to speak in the language of the business is not just about avoiding technology jargon. "That's just an obvious first step," he says. "We also look at terms like 'governance' and translate those into language that communicates their value to the business." Myers once heard a business colleague use "assurance" to describe governance. "As soon as I heard that, I loved it and that is the term we typically use now," he said. "Governance gets a reputation for being about standards and bureaucracy. When really, it should be about doing things in a repeatable way that helps make sure that everything performs well and is cost effective, reliable, and secure."

Another, more technical example is architecture. The members of my firm, gluttons for punishment that we are, have recruited an inordinate number of architects for our clients. The candidates we place into these roles run the gamut from the most deeply rooted technologist, who is kept hidden from the business at all costs, to the most strategic business thinker, who meets regularly with the senior leadership team. We can attest to Myers' contention that "If there are five billion people on the planet, there are probably five billion definitions of architecture."

So, rather than talk to his business partners about architecture, Myers discusses flexibility and adaptability. "It's not like I sit in a room and ponder what the right word is," says Myers. "When I'm having a conversation with a business person, I see their eyes light up when I hit on a certain word, like 'flexibility.' I realize that this term is resonating more than 'architecture.' So, my team and I begin to use the new word instead."

To reiterate: Language is powerful, and if you are not fully satisfied with the relationship your IT organization has with the rest of the business, you need to do something about it, including examining the language that you use. And if every time you say the word "infrastructure" or "cloud" or "agile" or "architecture" you hear a collective groan around the steering committee table, you should find a different word. There are hundreds of thousands of words in the English language. Surely you can find one that works.

Borrow your metaphors from the business

"In my industry, utilities, we have some great acronyms. We have SAIDI (system average interruption duration index) and SAIFI (system average interruption frequency index), to name only a few," says Doug Myers. "If you think about it, all we are really measuring is how often the power goes out and for how long. That same concept can apply to a server. Because those metrics work with the rest of the business, we are now using them in IT."

When Karla Viglasky, CIO of ITT Corporation, was at Honeywell, she found that her business partners had a lot of difficulty understanding the expense involved in building and delivering certain reports that her business partners used. "Everybody wants to push the button and get the report, and they don't understand what goes into that capability. They don't understand why it costs so much to push a button. I could get into ETLs and data cubes and loads, but I would lose their attention right away," she says. So Viglasky tried a number of different ways to communicate the complexity of data warehousing and finally found a metaphor that worked. "We are a manufacturing company, so I decided to talk about data as one of our products, like a pump or an engine," she says. "I told them, 'You need titanium to make your pump, but that titanium doesn't just fall out of the sky. People have to find the right materials and make sure that they match before delivering them.'" Most of Honeywell's business leaders know what it is like to explain the manufacturing process to their customers, so they could relate.

Change your name

Some CIOs find that modifying the name of their organization can be a powerful symbolic move toward change, and other CIOs are dead set against the idea. "I do not believe that the relationship between IT and other organizations is based on a name as much as it is based on how the organizations work together," says Denis Edwards, CIO of Manpower-Group. "I believe that it is the value the IT organization provides that makes a difference, not what it is called." Or, to quote a former GE CIO, "When I was at GE, we did rename some of the groups in IT. While I had no objections to this rebranding effort, I do not think it is central to the success of any IT organization. As the saying goes, 'A rose by any other name is still a rose.'" (Or was that Shakespeare?)

Heather Campbell feels differently. "In one of my CIO roles, the IT organization I inherited had been an underperforming organization called Business Information Technology Solutions, or BITS," says Campbell. "The running joke was that IT was surrounded by BullShit. In order to begin a transformation, I renamed the group 'Information Technology.' The key message that I gave to my IT staff was this: do you want to be associated with that old, disrespected, unproductive, underperforming organization? Or do you want to be a part of the new IT—proud, skilled professionals who deliver on their promises with quality?" To get the change to stick, Campbell told everyone that if they used the word BITS in front of her, she would charge them a dollar; she wound up collecting $160 for the United Way. "If I found it in writing, like in an emergency change request, I wouldn't approve the request because it came from an organization that didn't exist. It only took a couple of months before the word was no longer used."

Give your organization a motto

Under the assumption that words matter, Leslie Jones also adopted a motto for her organization: *We are in the business, our field just happens to be IT.* "There wasn't a meeting, a piece of written communication, a blog, anything that I did when this mantra wasn't the opening and closing statement," she says. "It was the phrase that I wanted on everybody's lips."

Now, some CIOs detest the use of mottos for organizations or programs. In their view, it is all about delivery and results. Others believe the most direct route toward unity with the rest of the business is not to develop a motto for IT alone, but to adopt the motto of the company. "We used to have a mission statement that was specific for IT," says Twila Day, CIO of Sysco, "but now we use our corporate mission statement: *To market and deliver great products to our customers with exceptional service.*"

But others, like Jones, have found that giving IT its own mantra is a powerful tool in bringing IT together with the business.

Steal This Motto

Much to my children's annoyance, my own personal motto is "I does what I likes and I likes what I does," but that probably won't work for you as CIO. Here are some that are working for others.

Business fast and simple: "Three words that describe everything that we want to be. It is about delivering solutions in three months, not three years. It is about not having an IT agenda, but lining up with the business agenda. It is about changing from a culture where we couldn't deliver a solution unless it was perfect." —Wayne Shurts, CIO of SUPERVALU

The Four Cs of Diamond IT: "Can Do, Communication, Consistency, and Commitment. Each "C" has a series of specific ways of delivering great IT service to our internal and external customers." —Brian Garavuso, CIO of Diamond Resorts International

Make it easy for TI to grow. —Brian Bonner, CIO of Texas Instruments

To deliver quality, innovative, and cost-effective solutions and services that help Atmos Energy achieve its objectives. —Rich Gius, CIO of Atmos Energy

Deliver technology at the speed of business: "This slogan captures the fact that the pace of business has quickened dramatically, much of it driven by the consumerization of IT. The traditional way of delivering IT services no longer works. We have to be faster, more flexible, more agile, and focused on bite-sized delivery that adds immediate and incremental value; if we do not, the business can pretty much do it without us, given how much easier it has become to build applications or acquire cloud services these days." —Lakshman Charanjiva, CIO of NextEra Energy, Inc./Florida Power & Light

Spread IT cheer: "Cheer starts with making sure people can rely on technology to meet their customers' requirements and ends when we fail to be their partner in solving business problems." —Carol Fineagan, CIO of EnergySolutions

Visibility—Integration—Consistency: —Sheryl Fikse, CIO of Southwire

Before you decide to remain in the crowd of curmudgeonly CIOs (you know who you are) who have decided that mottos are stupid, take a minute to think it through. We are entering an intense new world of computing, where the IT organization is going to be tested as it has never been tested before. Would the introduction of a motto give your team some focus during what promises to be dizzying times? Would a motto allow you to emphasize the two or three attributes you would like your IT organization to be known for? Is language change a leadership tool you might add to your belt?

Strengthen the Business Skills of your Team

So far in this chapter, we have focused alot on language as a potential bridge over that long-held divide between the business and IT. And, as an English major and journalist, I clearly have a bias when it comes to language as a powerful creator of change. But the divide between IT and the rest of the business is, in some companies, so ingrained that changing the language will not be enough. There is much more to do. One clear place to focus is your team, particularly those people who sit at the connection points between your organization and your peers.

Appoint business relationship executives

We touched briefly on the connection points between the business and IT in the last chapter, but because this set of professionals, those who straddle the business and IT, are so important to breaking the CIO paradox, we should spend a little more time on how to find, situate, and develop them. When Leslie Jones became CIO of Motorola Solutions, she found that the IT organization was cut along traditional lines, with functional groups running application development, infrastructure, and web design, and each group reaching out to the business as needed. This led to confusion on the part of her business partners, who started to wonder who, exactly, was in charge. "It was confusing and disorienting," says Jones. "So I decided that there will be one person and one person only who interfaces to a line of business. And that person will be seen as a member of the business's leadership team."

Jones made it clear to business leaders that this one person is the only IT person they will ever need to see, whether the issue is about strategy, a desktop, or a business system. Jones herself stays out of the relationship. "I make it a point of not allowing myself to intrude into those relationships," she says, "It is so critical that this person is seen by his business peers as the single point of power: knowledgeable, strategic, and committed to impeccable delivery."

Think carefully about reporting structure

The reporting structure that has worked best for Kevin Horner, who recently retired as CIO of Alcoa, is to have the IT leaders who are serving specific businesses report directly into those businesses, with a dotted line to the CIO. "This is from spending thirty years in a company where the business unit was king," he says. "If the person serving the business is not being measured by the business and is not on the same compensation plans as the business, the relationship will not work. If those people report directly to the CIO, they will never develop the detailed understanding of the business. It will never become innate."

But whatever you do, avoid making the role a toothless one. As Tom Farrah discussed in more detail in chapter 1, the key is to give accountability for project delivery to the relationship managers, rather than appoint them as "liaisons" and "translators" who have to rely on the kindness of centralized delivery organizations to get anything done.

But whatever reporting structure you choose, you need to find that bilingual person who can keep one foot in the business and one foot in IT. What is at play with these roles is a particularly challenging CIO Paradox: *The very traits and skills that make some people great technologists often make them not so great with business relationships.* When it comes to people with deep technology skills, there is some heavy-duty DNA at work that is going to dictate their interpersonal skills. Still, there are actions you can take to mitigate the challenge.

If you do not have an effective way of teaching business skills to your technology team, like rotating them through the business, start a program now. Take it from a recruiter: it is hard to find ready-made talent with great technology and business skills. These candidates are out there, but it will cost you time and money to recruit them. The more bilingual talent you can cultivate yourself, the more successful you will be as an IT organization. And when you export these valuable people out to the business, you will create a culture that is knowledgeable about IT and you will be one step closer to breaking the paradox. Kevin Hart, CTO and CIO of Cox Communications, gives a great example of his approach to growing blended leaders in chapter 9. Here are some other ideas.

Use the buddy system

Like most CIOs, Colleen Wolf, CIO of Ventura Foods, has leaders of applications, infrastructure, PMO, and enterprise architecture in her organization. The roles are not business specific; they each serve all of the company's business functions. Even so, Wolf assigns each IT leader in her organization to a partner on the business side, regardless of what projects or programs they are working on. "My head of infrastructure partners with the head of business operations. My head of enterprise architecture partners with HR. My PMO partners with finance," she says. Wolf tells the business leaders that she would like her leaders in IT to be involved with their departments on a regular basis, to come to the staff meetings and learn that particular function. "IT is often isolated because nobody knows who we are and what we are here for," she says. "But by aligning my IT leadership team with business executives, we are establishing transparency in both directions. We are creating a dialogue. We are getting off the island."

Educate your people

There are so many ways to give business acumen to your staff. One widely practiced approach is to find smart people in the business who have a healthy aptitude for and appreciation of IT, and entice them into your organization. Another is to take your smart IT people and educate them about the business. "We worked with a local college to develop a multi-year program that trained our customer-facing teams and our managers in how to listen to the business, talk to the business, and really understand what they were saying," says Motorola Solutions's Leslie Jones. "We put a real focus on how our IT leaders can change their communication style to be appropriate to the person they were talking with."

Be careful when you rotate people

When Heather Campbell arrived as the new CIO at Canadian Pacific Railway, she found that there were a few IT people working in audit, one of whom was one of the most credentialed security people she had ever met. "I asked him, 'What are you doing in audit?' and he told me that audit is where he was placed as a high-potential employee so that he could learn the business." Campbell characterized audit as "purgatory," and moved him out. "You can't blindly give business experience to your people," she says. "You run the risk of losing them by trying to make them something that they're not."

Back in 1998, when Campbell was finishing her MBA, she was director of enterprise network solutions for a major bank. This was a deeply technical engineering role. Campbell says, "When I went to my boss and said, 'I have my MBA, what's next,' she said, 'We see you in a sales role. You'll be very competitive there.' Well, working in sales is my own personal version of hell, so within four months of that conversation, I left the company for an IT job, and I've never looked back."

Enlist your business leaders

Karla Viglasky asks ITT's presidents to come to her team meetings and give presentations on what is happening in their businesses. "My top fifty people will be meeting in Miami next week, and the leaders of all of the functions we interact with will be there," she says. We tend to think a lot about how to organize IT so that it is embedded in the business, but it works in the other direction as well. "I am trying to bring 'the business' to IT," says Viglasky. "Our business leaders become more knowledgeable about our strategy in IT and my people get smarter about the business."

Viglasky also starts all of her team meetings with an update on the business. "I just call our communications person and ask for the latest update on the business," she says. "Regardless of how many projects we are working on, I spent a few minutes on what's happening with our company. It is an easy way to flow a little business knowledge into the IT organization."

Initiate a company-wide program

When Bill Krivoshik joined Time Warner, he enrolled in a company-sponsored program designed to teach the business to senior executives. "It is a wonderful set of programs where you pretend that it is your job to manage all of the Time Warner businesses for three years," says Krivoshik. "'When should I release this movie? What should I do about the ratings? How will the networks react to this decision?'" The program includes a great deal of interaction among the leaders from across the company and is a creative and efficient way to teach the business to new executives. "Having attended that program, I understand the major levers of the business now," he says. If you have been waiting too long for your company to develop a program to teach the business to your IT people, leverage your business relationships and build one yourself.

Teach negotiating skills

At Pepco Holdings all support services, including IT, go through a training model that draws much of its material from *Getting to Yes: Negotiating Agreement without Giving In* by Roger Fisher, William Ury, and Bruce Patton. Based on the work of the Harvard Negotiation Project, *Getting to Yes* is a step-by-step methodology for finding mutually acceptable agreements in a variety of contexts. (And for IT organizations, which often have the stigma of saying only "no," the ability to say "yes" comes in handy.) "It is the most important business book I've ever read," says Pepco CIO Doug Myers.

Peter Weis, CIO of Matson Navigation uses a different book as the basis for his negotiation training. "One of the most important books I've read is *Bargaining for Advantage: Negotiation Strategies for Reasonable People* by G. Richard Shell," he says. "This book was written by a Wharton professor and guides me in my own executive relationships." CIOs train their teams on project management, quality assurance, and requirements definition but they do not always spend time on negotiation skills. Given how much of your money goes to vendors, and how important business relationships are to the IT organization, it is critical that your people know how to negotiate. "This book gives you a great framework with detailed examples and lets you develop your own personal point of view on how to negotiate," says Weis. "It is mandatory reading for my entire senior management team, and we do a whole off-site training program based on the book.

Your Reading List

In 2000, I directed the CIO Best Practice Exchange, an online network of Fortune 500 CIOs who posted comments about a variety of topics. One of the most active discussions was around perennial leadership books that CIOs have relied on for mentoring and in their own professional development. What I should have done then (but, hey, I had toddlers at the time!) was to make a list of those books to share with other CIOs. I would like the opportunity to redeem myself now. Having polled our network of CIOs, I submit herewith (albeit twelve years later) CIOs' observations about the leadership books they love the most:

Steve Jobs by Walter Isaacson: "I recently finished Steve Jobs' biography, and my wife commented that it was the first time in a long time that I have talked so much about a book. One of the things I admire about Jobs was how engaged and involved he was in everything Apple did. He had a vision and he also had specific ideas on how that vision should come to life. I think many of us as CIOs have convinced ourselves that details are not something we should be involved in, but I have always felt details matter and that they provide the most valuable coaching moments."   —Denis Edwards, CIO of ManpowerGroup

"I have been focusing on how to gain efficiencies and output by optimizing teams, and can recommend two books on that topic: *Co-Active Coaching: Transforming Business, Transforming Lives* by Karen Kimsey-House, Henry Kimsey-House, and Phillip Sandahl and *Emotional Intelligence* by Daniel Goleman; Goleman's book sets the foundation for the importance of EI and has an assessment for benchmarking people in relationship to their peer group." —Karin Catton, CIO of Norgren

"Any CIO interested in driving business model innovation for their companies should read *Business Model Generation: A Handbook for Visionaries, Game Changers, and Challengers* by Alexander Oster-walder."   —Werner Boeing, CIO of Roche Diagnostics

"Two books that have influenced me greatly are Garry Wills' *Lincoln at Gettysburg* and David McCullough's *Truman*. They are very different books, but both convey a strong message of servant leadership, plainspoken truthtelling, and unwavering perseverance." —Daniel Barchi, CIO Yale New Haven Health System

"There are four books I use when I teach our IT Leadership Development course:

Good to Great by Jim Collins: I think this is the best business book written to date. It is simple and well researched with actionable approaches to solving real-world problems.

Raise the Bar by Mike Vance: This teaches you how to think out of the box from the person who actually coined the term "thinking out of the box."

World Class IT by Peter High: This book works well with *Good to Great* but it more specifically addresses the IT function.

The Structure of Scientific Revolutions by Thomas Kuhn: This may be one of the most important books written in the last fifty years, but is a book almost no one has heard of. I actually changed majors in college after reading this book. This is a philosophy book that first described the concept of "paradigm shifts." It is critical for IT people to understand this. It is the key to understanding how disruptive technologies work, and how basic science evolves over time. This is a very heady book, and I usually put it in to make people really think. When you read this, you really understand the basis of how change happens."

—Gregory Fell, CIO of Terex

"I actually like *Managing Humans: Biting and Humorous Tales of a Software Engineering Manager* by Michael Lopp: It offers a clear approach to teaching management and leadership skills to technical people. I also like *It's Your Ship: Management Techniques from the Best Damn Ship in the Navy* by Michael Abrashoff as an accessible way to focus on what you *can* do to move things forward in situations where you don't have direct authority or control over all aspects of the situation."   —Michelle Garvey, CIO of Warnaco

The Big Switch: Rewiring the World from Edison to Google by Nicolas Carr: "It offers a peek into the future of technology."   —Mike Blake, CIO of Hyatt Hotels

The Goal: A Process of Ongoing Improvement by Eliyahu Goldratt: "I first read this book in 1988 and have bought hundreds of copies for my teams. It's a very quick read that reads as a story and offers a teaching opportunity about strategy, drive, direction, and how to create followership. How many times do we get started on a project not really knowing what success looks like? The other is *LL Bean: The Making of an American Icon* by Leon Gorman, chairman of the company and grandson of the founder. I was given this book as a gift, because I love all things Maine, and when I read it, I decided to buy copies for my team. It is the story of a wonderfully strong brand that had lost its way and recovered to become even stronger. It relates to IT because it is a perfect example of a value system that is all about customer service, and they mean it in everything that they do." —Sue Kozik, CIO of Independence Blue Cross

Conclusion

In 1999, I wrote a column for *CIO* magazine called, "Why Does Everyone Hate the IS Department?" Some choice quotes from the sources I interviewed include, "We get constant calls about problems that we know for a fact we've explained to users time and time again. Everyone wants to use their computers, but nobody is willing to learn how." And "Many IS organizations preserve this 'We're gods' attitude. IS workers are often resistant to working in teams, and they often don't give users proper training on the systems they impose on them. They just say, 'Here, use it.'"

I realize that the sentiments expressed in that article are a thing of the past in many IT organizations. But in others, they are alive and well. What differentiates the first group from the second? Why is it that some CIOs have broken the "IT and the Business" Paradox and have completely done away with the "us and them" mentality? In these organizations, phrases like "IT and the business" make as little sense as "the daughter and the family." Do the IT professionals in those organizations have different DNA? Were they raised better? Are the company's employees more understanding and patient when it comes to IT?

I don't think so. The CIOs who have broken the "IT and the Business"

Paradox spend time and energy on communication and language and training and relationships; those activities are as important to them as running their infrastructure. They have a vision for the way they want IT to be perceived and the ability to battle the natural order of things and embed IT in the business. Lord knows it isn't easy, when IT demand is greater than supply and security threats are growing and computer science grads are decreasing and consumerization is completely changing the ground underneath your feet. But if changing the name of the IT organization and or assigning a new book to your leadership team can get you one step further on the journey toward bringing IT closer to the business, then do it. You may be able to get past this troublesome paradox once and for all. Your takeaways:

- *Pay attention to language:* In your reports, your meetings, your conversations, and your titles. Language is one of the most powerful tools you have (and it's cheap); be sure you are using it.
- *Improve your staff's knowledge of the business:* You don't have to send them to business school when you have business executives all around you. Find a way to harness the knowledge of your colleagues to give better business acumen to your team.
- *Embed your people in the business:* Most CIOs are reorganizing from a traditional plan, deliver, run model to a structure of mini-CIOs each accountable for IT strategy and delivery to one major business area. If you haven't done this yet, it may be time for a reorg.

Stakeholder Relationship Journey Assessment

My good friends at the CIO Executive Council have been generous enough to lend me their Stakeholder Relationship Journey tool, a quick self-assessment intended to gauge your IT organization's relationship with the executive committee, line of business heads, and other peers. While we are on the subject of "IT and the business" you may want to take this assessment to determine just how strong your ties to the business are.

Check the box for each point that is *routinely and typically* true for a *large majority* of the stakeholders in your organization.

In general, our enterprise stakeholders typically and routinely...

- ☐ Have a reasonable understanding of the benefits, risks and limitations of information technology
- ☐ Perceive IT as a sound investment relative to other capital spending
- ☐ Trust us with discretionary funds to use for the betterment of the business
- ☐ Involve us in the enterprise budgeting process
- ☐ See us as the preferred service provider for strategic applications
- ☐ Proactively seek our advice on technology to enable their initiatives
- ☐ Perceive us less as a separate service provider and more as an integral part of the enterprise
- ☐ Publicly acknowledge our strategic importance to their particular unit, area or function
- ☐ Consider the CIO as an enterprise stakeholder just like the other heads of units/functions
- ☐ Appreciate and respect the CIO's role in identifying cross-enterprise challenges/solutions
- ☐ Understand and appreciate our role in transforming enterprise operations
- ☐ Proactively seek our advice on process transformation
- ☐ Engage us in strategic discussions about the end-customer experience/client-facing services
- ☐ Involve our senior IT leaders—not just the CIO—in strategic decision-making

☐ Engage us in decision-making discussions outside of formal executive- or steering-committee meetings

☐ See us as a source of talent to hire into non-IT roles in their own organizations

☐ Proactively seek our advice and contributions for their innovation and differentiation initiatives

☐ Act on innovation ideas originating with our CIO or IT organization

☐ See us as a primary source of ideas for new enterprise opportunities

☐ Have entrusted our CIO to lead a revenue- or operations-related unit or function in addition to IT

Scoring: Add the total number of checked boxes above to determine your cumulative score:_____

Scoring Analysis: The CIO Executive Council recommends in its "Future-State CIO Journey" concept (council.cio.com/futurestate) that to deliver maximum value and remain relevant, CIOs must elevate the relationship from the level of provider to partner to ultimately, peer. Your final score demonstrates where you currently stand on the journey.

1–7 = Service Provider

Your IT organization has moved away from the "cost center" perception and now seen by most stakeholders as a service provider, with established IT credibility based on running the IT function with efficiency and effectiveness. To get to the next level, IT must focus its leadership enterprisewide and cultivate collaborative relationships with stakeholders, which will establish IT's influence in transforming the enterprise.

8–13 = IT Partner

Your IT organization is seen as a trusted IT partner to the enterprise, with an enterprisewide focus and the power to influence the stakeholders. To get to the next level, IT must focus its leadership externally on end customers and the marketplace to build greater business (vs. IT) credibility, which will enable IT to engage as a peer in client-facing strategy.

14–18 = Business Peer

Your IT organization is seen as a true enterprise peer, with all the business credibility you need to engage in developing and driving enterprise strategy. To master and build on this, IT must bring innovation and customer-facing differentiation ideas to the table, execute flawlessly, and establish its reputation as a game changer.

19–20 = Game Changer

Your organization is seen as a game changer, and is in a rare position to drive the competitive future of the enterprise. Consider volunteering to be a leadership case study or a coach to share your experience.

For more Information on the Council and Future-State CIO® Journey, contact cec_info@cio.com

6

The Accountability versus Ownership Paradox

As CIO, your role is to work with the rest of the executive committee to define the direction and goals of the business. You articulate that business strategy to your IT organization and develop a strategic plan to drive and support it. Once your IT strategy is set, you and your team develop programs and projects to execute against the plan, gain funding, and implement the projects. It is all very sensible and straightforward.

Most CIOs have little trouble with the first part: assessing the goals of the business, developing and articulating an IT strategy, and getting funding approval. But many fall short of actually getting their partners in the business to engage in the execution of that IT strategy. As one CIO said to me recently, getting business partners to do their part in implementing IT is like "pushing a rope." One would think that business leaders who have agreed upon a set of IT investments would recognize how important it is for them to step up and implement them. But given their own priorities and resource constraints, they do not always do their part.

I have heard many a CIO stand up at a conference and proudly proclaim, "In my company, there are no IT projects, only business projects."

Those are nice words, but when the project is complete and someone, somewhere, isn't happy with the results, it is the CIO who is left holding the bag, not the business partner. Or, as Heather Campbell, former CIO of Canadian Pacific, recalls, "My former boss used to say, 'There are only two types of projects: business successes and IT failures.'"

A business-led steering committee may agree on the strategy, the investment, and the plan for execution, but business leaders do not always sustain their participation through the entire life cycle of the project. This is the "last mile of alignment," where the CIO has the somewhat daunting task of getting his business peers to pony up resources to support the implementation through to the end. This paradoxical situation puts the CIO in the "accountability without authority" spot, which is never a fun place to be. The paradox more formally stated: *You are accountable for the success of a project, but the business has to own it.*

Despite the plethora of books and articles and conferences about IT working productively with business partners to deliver IT solutions, executives in many companies still perceive large technology projects as the responsibility of IT. Why, after all this time, is this still the case?

Steve Ambrose, CIO of DTE Energy, believes that much of the project ownership challenge stems from the fact that IT is a very young profession being asked to grow up quickly. "Decades ago, the delivery of IT projects was much simpler than it is today," says Ambrose. "Delivering IT was more like building a warehouse, where the business could specify square feet and other basic requirements, and IT would deliver a discrete new piece of technology."

Today, with IT's high level of integration—where automating one process impacts every other process and IT is embedded across the enterprise—technology implementation relies on a whole different skill set. "What we find is the need for good change management skills among a professional community that has been known for building warehouses," says Ambrose. "The business says, 'I don't know why you guys make your stuff so difficult' and IT winds up in the position of having to defend itself against uninformed accusations." Both IT and the business are still haunted by the old perception that delivering IT is simple, and both sides wind up frustrated and disappointed. "This swing from simple discrete work to integrated change management, people, and process work creates the need for a very different skill set in IT people and a very different relationship between IT and the business," Ambrose says.

Don't Mistake Governance for Shared Accountability

All CIOs know that in order to share accountability for IT projects, they need to establish viable governance structures. But it is a mistake to believe that good governance alone will ensure project success. "For most companies, governance is just a series of committees that people hide behind," says Jeanne Ross, director of MIT's Center for Information Systems Research. "In trying to get everyone involved, governance can become an obstacle to clear accountability." Michelle Garvey, CIO of global apparel leader Warnaco, agrees. When it comes to shared accountability for project delivery, "Governance is necessary but not sufficient," she says. "You are a fool if you believe that steering committees are going to guarantee success."[4]

Have the conversation

Part of the challenge in sharing accountability for IT delivery with your business partners is the natural tendency for corporate environments to be political. "Success has many fathers, and failure is an orphan," says Kumud Kalia, CIO of Akamai Technologies. "People are always trying to point the finger at someone, and they will choose the person who has less political power." To preempt the finger pointing, Kalia suggests you act fast when you take on a new CIO role in establishing yourself as something other than a second-class citizen. "When you are the new person, you usually have about a hundred days to establish your bona fides," he says. "This is the time to set the boundaries and decide with your executive peers who is accountable for what."

While there is a whole industry based around how to set up effective governance structures to ensure collective accountability, Kalia suggests you have some honest conversations before you start building committees and PMOs. "Go to your stakeholders in the executive committee and have a frank conversation about who gets to decide what and who is responsible for what, so that there is no confusion," he says. "If you don't get agreement at that level, then governance and all of the structures around it simply become avoidance mechanisms. Before you establish committees, just start with simple words."

Soon after ITT Corporation was spun off from ITT Industries, the company needed a new payroll system, and the HR organization told Karla Viglasky, CIO, which tool they wanted to use. "I said, 'Hold on a minute, IT needs to be involved in that decision,' and in the very first meeting they said, 'Okay, Karla. You own this project now, right?'"

While Steve Ambrose credits some of the challenges of IT execution with the fact that change management is a relatively new skill, Viglasky sees it differently. According to her, it is precisely because IT organizations are good at change and project management that IT so often winds up being held accountable when projects go south. "It is in our DNA to be good project managers because we think in a linear way, so our business partners' tendency is to lay the entire project at our door," she says.

In order to avoid full accountability for the payroll project, Viglasky sat down with the CFO and HR leader and had a candid conversation about the project and about how IT, HR, and finance needed to work together on it. "There was no way I was going to run that project," she says. In order to make her business partners understand, she used an analogy. "I explained to them that just because IT is a part of the project, it does not mean that IT should run it. Suppose you have a problem with your car, and I'm a chemical engineer. There are certainly chemicals in your car. Does that mean that I should fix it?"

Good governance and project management offices may be tools in ensuring a true partnership between IT and business leaders, but they are not enough. Steering committees and rules of engagement and prioritization plans will not work if there is not honest, simple agreement about roles and responsibilities at the beginning. "I have seen the 'two in a box' concept work, and I have seen it fail," says Viglasky, referring to the notion that every project should have two leaders—one from IT and one from another function—at every level of a project. "It fails when it's a ruse, when it's just for show. It's when the CIO says, 'We're two in a box!' and the business partner is just sitting there drinking coffee. I can drag my CEO around with me all I want. But if two in a box isn't real, you'll fail even bigger than if you just did the project on your own."

The key is to have the honest conversation early on, just as Viglasky did at the beginning of the payroll project. "I'm an introvert, and because we had just spun off, I did not know these executives well at all," she says. "It was not the easiest thing for me to have a frank conversation like that. But after we all sat down and agreed to partner on the project, the steering committees worked well and the project began to go more smoothly."

Work the social network

Michelle Garvey spends a fair amount of time monitoring the "buzz" that tends to run around a company during a major transformative project. "When you are in the middle of a big project, you need to keep your ear to the ground," she says. "You need to understand the noise—what people are saying about a project. You cannot just accept the communication that takes place during the steering committee." Garvey is not a direct report of the CEO, but her business sponsors often are. "They are in the CEO's staff meeting every week and talking about our projects, but I am not in the room," she says. "I have my own individual relationships with members of the senior executive team. They tell me what's going on. This way, I can be aware of any issues before our formal meetings. If you go into a formal meeting without already knowing about a problem, you are vulnerable and naïve."

Hire a third party project manager

At Warnaco, Garvey and a business partner were in the middle of a project and had differing perspectives on whether the project was ready to go live. Garvey believed the project had not been adequately tested and her business partner disagreed. So they hired a third party project manager to do a "project readiness" audit and bring in an outside perspective. "If you have a risky and contentious project, a third party can be useful. This person reported both to the business president and to me. We both knew him and trusted him; he had credibility."

Involve the right people in the discussion

When everyone has general agreement about accountability, governance does play an important role in keeping all parties on the same page. For Annabelle Bexiga, CIO of TIAA-CREF, the most important element of good governance is getting the right people at the table. "We make sure that we have senior people from IT and the other parts of the business," she says. "If you have the real decision makers at the meetings, that's when you can truly establish transparency and talk about projects in a direct way. If one of our core projects is behind schedule, we can get at the heart of what the problem is. You make decisions as a team and avoid the perception that IT has dropped the ball."

Don't separate out IT governance at all

Brent Stacey, CIO of Idaho National Laboratory, is not a big fan of IT governance models. "The governance of IT should be integrated into the governance of the company or institution," he says. When Stacey stepped into his current CIO role, he dismantled the IT steering committee. "I told them that if they would not abolish their IT governance model, I was not their man," he says. "Most companies have IT governance because technology is expensive and CEOs think you need a special watch group for it. But my belief is IT governance just makes the problem worse by keeping IT removed from the rest of the business." At Idaho National Laboratory, there is one governance structure for all functions across the enterprise. The governance structure is supported by three councils—operations, science and technology, and management—of which all report to an executive council. The management council includes leaders from legal, HR, supply chain, finance, independent audit, and IT, with Stacey as the chair. "The deputy CIO represents IT on the management council," he says, "because I need to maintain independence." The CIO is a member of all three councils, and the chairs of these councils all attend the executive council. This way IT is fully integrated into the governance structure of the organization.

Let the Business Lead

As many CIOs have learned the hard way, large programs that are led entirely by IT are almost certain to fail. "When you start thinking about the big programs, programs that drive real change, you have to be sure those are led by the business," says Leslie Jones, CIO of Motorola Solutions.

But getting the business to lead an IT project can be like getting my daughters to do their own laundry. I teach them to do it, I give them incentives to do it, I model the behavior, I even yell at them, but they won't lift a finger, and the laundry that piles up at the door is my problem. (Note: at the time of this writing, we are piloting a new program to get my daughters to do their laundry involving threats of limiting their social activity. I will provide an update in a future edition of *The CIO Paradox*.)

"One of the problems that I often see in IT organizations is that CIOs believe IT should lead from the front," says Jones. "That may make you feel good when you talk with your peers at CIO conferences, but it rarely produces the business results that you had hoped for. The business is never going to embrace a program that involves significant change if they don't feel in truth that it is business led. You're much better off if you lead from the middle, put your business partners out front, and then back them up."

So here we run into an interesting CIO Paradox: *CIOs need to have egos that are big enough to initiate transformative projects but small enough to let someone else take the credit.* Striking the balance between the chutzpah necessary to lead IT and the humility it takes to be successful at it is tough, and not everyone can do it.

Pick the right leader

"It is a common mistake among less experienced CIOs to believe that all business partners are interchangeable," says Jones. "Left alone, the business will give you the mediocre but reliable person who has never rocked any boats, where taking them out of their current role and putting them on this program is not much of a loss."

Your challenge, then, is to build on the trust you've established through consistent delivery and negotiate for the business leader who commands deep and profound respect among her peers.

Ralph Loura, CIO of The Clorox Company, learned the importance of choosing the right sponsor the hard way. "When I was in my first CIO role, we were delivering a huge CRM project and the VP of sales operations was the project sponsor. We built requirements for the project, and delivered it on time, on spec, and on budget. It was so perfect it made you weep. We built great functionality around opportunity management and the deals desk. And it was connected to the marketing channel. It was just beautiful. We rolled it out and in the first week we had something like a 2 percent adoption rate. The field refused to use the tool. We were devastated."

The problem was that the VP of sales operations had sponsored the perfect solution to allow his sales team to spend two or three hours a day doing detailed forecasting and rolling the numbers up to him so that he had the information he needed. But the sales people had no interest in spending their time that way, so they did not use the tool. "We designed the perfect system to meet the requirements," says Loura, "but it completely missed the mark."

There are two lessons to be learned from Loura's tale of woe:

- The choosers are not the users: "You always have to remember the difference between the users and the choosers." The chooser, in this case, was the VP of sales operations. "We listened to him," says Loura, "but we lost sight of the users. We never thought about how we were going to get the salespeople to be excited about the technology."
- Talk to everyone: "Regardless of who your sponsor is, don't take your advice in terms of platform or strategy or value creation from one source," says Loura. "Make sure you have built broad alliances throughout the business. When it comes to delivering value, don't pin your hopes and dreams to one executive leader. Make sure you're checking with other functions to anticipate the downstream effects of what one leader wants."

Back up your leader

Once you have the right business leader signed on to the project, someone who is respected by the business and plugged into the user base, you need to back her up. "You have to make absolutely certain that the leader succeeds, and that means taking on a lot of the back office, project management tactics necessary to get the program done," says Leslie Jones. "Whenever anybody sends a note out to the general population, whenever anybody talks about the program, that leader should be up there as your spokesperson. You may be pulling the wires behind the scenes, but the program has to look like it's totally business led."

Accept the fact that you will not get all the credit

Personally, I love getting credit. I still want my *CIO* magazine editor to send me roses when I submit a new column each month, and I am slightly disappointed when my husband doesn't congratulate me at the end of every day for completing a full day of work. I can only imagine how difficult it is for CIOs to achieve some fairly astounding feats like delivering a new suite of mobile applications (or even upgrading ERP!) and not be handed the keys to the city. Hence, the paradox: *You drive the project from the backseat, a paradox unto itself, and when the project is a success, the business gets the credit.* Ah, but that is the lot in life of the CIO. (You asked for the job.)

Lead the Business

As a manager, you are always deciding when you should lead an initiative and when you should hand the reins to members of your senior team. The same goes with parenting: When is it best that you drive the car, and when do you allow your new teenage driver to take the wheel? Your ability to harness those mentoring instincts comes in handy when engaging the business in IT project execution.

Bring your business leaders along

"As CIO, my job is to lead my IT organization in teaching business leaders what it means to own the project, and we educate them about what their environment will be like once the project is complete," says Jody Davids, CIO of Best Buy. "It is our responsibility to teach while we are executing, and to bring the business along, IT alone cannot own the project." Davids uses an analogy to explain her approach.

"When I wanted to remodel my house, I knew I couldn't do it myself, so I hired an architect," says Davids. "I was the owner of the house, and

I was going to pay for it and live in it when the project was done. But the architect had to understand what I needed, so he spent time with me, and asked me questions, and I had to spend the time with him. I couldn't just hand him a page ripped out of a magazine and say, 'Build me this.'"

Once Davids and the architect had spent time talking through her goals for the house, she hired a general contractor to do the work. "When the general contractor reached a stopping point because it looked like something was not going to work the way we planned it, he had to pause and explain the problem to me, and we had to talk through options in terms of usability, appearance, cost, and timeline. I owned the project, but the architect and the contractor had to bring me along. And they had to educate me about what it would be like to live in the house once it is built."

Hold your horses

Here is a CIO Paradox for you: CIOs have a bias for action. They respect deadlines and they want results. Their teams do too. They can't wait to get started, and their business partners are eager as well. Let's get the show on the road! Because of this collective need for speed, and because budgets and deadlines are so tight, CIOs sometimes bow to pressure and move too quickly to get to the end. "We sometimes plow through a project in the spirit of checking it off the list as being on time and on budget," says Davids. "We do not always take the time to bring our clients along," says Davids.

Colleen Wolf, CIO of Ventura Foods, agrees. "CIOs and their IT teams like to get things done," says Wolf. "They are in a hurry to demonstrate value. Especially when CIOs take on a new role, they know that they are under the gun, so they initiate projects that should not be initiated by IT. They get out over their skis. They think, 'Okay, so the business isn't as engaged as we would like them to be. We can solve for that. We'll work it out. Let's start looking at vendors.'" But without shared accountability with an active, invested, and engaged set of business partners, an IT-enabled business project is doomed. "Projects are won or lost at the beginning," says Wolf. "If you don't structure the project, at its start, so that your business partners are leading it, the project is destined to fail.

Refuse to start the project

If the project is important enough for the company to fund, it is important enough to justify the time and attention of your business partners. "I will refuse to start a project until a leader from the relevant part of the business is assigned," says Heather Campbell, of BasicallyIT. "For a CRM project, you need leaders from customer service and from the sales force to lead the project, and you need people in their organizations on the ground, who are involved in the day-to-day activities. If you don't have that, you shouldn't start. Or else you are doomed."

Charge the business for IT

As I was conducting interviews for this book, I probably heard the word "transparency" more than any other. When I am asked to recruit a CIO because the incumbent has not fared too well, one of the complaints I hear most often from the business is "IT costs alot but we never know where the money goes." As Kevin Horner, former CIO of Alcoa, puts it, "This IT stuff costs a lot, and CIOs have not done themselves any favors by creating a big black box that no one can understand." Management studies have shown that people accept decisions that are not in their favor if they can see how the decision was made. The same goes for IT: everyone will be happier if they have some understanding of costs, cost drivers, and what they, as consumers, can control.

For Kevin Horner, the clear and effective way to make business leaders accountable for IT is to charge them for it. "We established a services business and billed 95 percent of IT costs back to the consumers of those services," he says. "Our services fit on a rate card that is one sheet of paper, with a series of levers that the business can pull to impact whether the costs go up or down. Do you want the people in the plants to have Internet access? Do you want print services? It's their business, and they can decide."

The key to making the nearly 100 percent services model work, says Horner, is to make sure the consumers of IT understand market benchmarks for the services you are providing. "Part of operational excellence is to allow them to compare your costs to the costs on the street," he says. "The only I way I know how to get those benchmarks is to put your environment out for bid and let the supply side tell you about your cost structure." To Horner, a CIO should strive for a scenario in which nearly 100 percent of IT costs are borne by the consumers of IT services, with just a few policy items accounted as corporate overhead. "If you're at less than 90 percent, you are not transparent, and you will have little credibility with the business," he says.

Conclusion

In many ways, the "accountability without ownership" paradox is the most foundational of all of the CIO paradoxes. When my firm is asked to replace a CIO who has been asked to leave a company, it is frequently because he has not found a way out of this conundrum. The ERP program fails, and the CIO is fired. But, how *do* you drive a car from the back seat? How do you share accountability with a business partner who reports to the CEO, when you do not? How do you push a rope? Solving this paradox is tough sledding, to be sure, but CIOs are doing it every day.

- *Establish cognitive dissonance:* Like so many aspects of the CIO role, the key to solving this particular paradox is credibility. If your business partners believe that you, as CIO, are someone who delivers on your promises, hires and manages good people, and has the goals of the business as your beacon, you will not be left "holding the bag" when projects run amok. Warnaco's Michelle Garvey uses the concept of "cognitive dissonance" to describe the reaction she works hard to build among the business. "When someone in the company says that IT is useless, or failing, or unresponsive, I want the general reaction among the rest of the company to be, 'Wait, that can't be right; I know our IT organization, and this cannot be their fault. If everyone knows our reputation for delivery, we will get the benefit of the doubt, and I will have the opportunity to get ahead of the problem," she says.

- *Assess your credibility:* Are you continually over committing and counting on business resources that turn out not to be there? Are your estimates often inaccurate? Do you regularly suffer from scope creep? A solid track record is an essential ingredient to establishing the cognitive dissonance that Garvey describes. Do you have one?

- *Assess your business leadership:* Do an inventory of your major IT initiatives. Do they all have business leaders? Do those business leaders have the necessary credibility to lead? Are they devoting enough time and attention to the program? Or are you actually leading the project? If you have wound up the de facto product sponsor (which happens all the time in IT), you are not in a good place. Act now to engage a business leader to whom you can pass the baton.

PART III

Your Staff: They Just Don't Make Them Like That

7

The Recruiting Paradox

Way back in 2000, just before the dot-com bust, I was writing a weekly column for CIO.com and I spent months covering "the technology work-force crisis." The big issue was the cap that the U.S. government had put on H-1B visas and the strong need that companies had for developers and other technologists. Then along came the dot-com bust, and the news (and my column) was all about layoffs and identifying the real goats in the Internet debacle.

As the economy recovered from the bust, we all took a more balanced view of technology hiring. Companies needed good technology people, and they were able to recruit them pretty easily or augment their teams offshore.

Enter the 2010s. With cloud and mobility and consumerization, companies are in even greater need of technology talent than they were in the late 1990s, and that talent is in even shorter supply. "Experienced mobile architect" is an oxymoron, and yet you really need one. And so do all of your competitors.

One approach to ending your technology talent woes is to build talent development programs and grow your own. Another is to get really good at recruiting. Sounds easy: hire a team of recruiters and get cracking. Or hire a trusted recruiting partner and "outsource" the problem. In theory, the solution is a simple one, but in practice, it buckles under a paradox all its own: *CIOs are experts at business process change, but they have not done much to change the process of recruiting.* If you are having trouble recruiting technology people at any level, from developers to SVPs, there is a reason, and I am guessing it is embedded in your recruiting process.

So, we'll begin at the beginning and walk through the stages of a search. Just for fun, let's talk about the mistakes CIOs sometimes make during each phase and what they might do to correct them. But before we get started, I would like to be clear that many of my firm's clients (you know who you are) have fabulous, efficient, first-rate recruiting processes. They launch searches which, despite the inherent challenge of recruiting people with technical, communication, business, and leadership skills, are successful. These CIOs have figured out what so many still need to understand: recruiting is one of the most important activities you can perform for your company. The process deserves as much time and attention as anything else you do.

Requirements Definition

Just as with IT projects, recruiting projects are won or lost at the beginning. The more time devoted to planning, stakeholder analysis, and requirements definition, the more successful the project.

Beware the purple squirrel

One of the greatest obstacles to a good search is in the way some CIOs define the roles they would like to recruit. They define their senior positions based on what they need, not on the career paths that people actually follow. I would love to hire someone to do my hair, feed my children, manage my database, and drywall the basement. But workers don't come like that.

Several years ago, I was approached by a CIO in manufacturing to recruit an enterprise architect leader who would report to the PMO. For political reasons, this CIO felt that he needed to give his PMO leader an additional functional responsibility, and he did not want to add another direct report to his own leadership team. Plus, he had already budgeted the role at the director level, not the VP level. As much as I would have loved to take on this new client, we had to turn the search down (something that goes against every sinew of my being). I had learned, after filling many enterprise architecture positions, that the structure would never fly. Good enterprise architects do not want to report into the PMO. They worry that they will live in the projects and never be able to perform the real work of enterprise architecture. I ran into that CIO recently; he had filled the role, but the person did not work out and he was at it again.

The way the purple squirrel manifests most often is in a CIO's desire to hire someone who is both strategic and technical at the same time. Last year, we did a search for a consumer packaged goods CIO who was looking to hire a business intelligence leader. The candidate needed to have the director-level experience of selling business intelligence as a concept across multiple lines of business; at the same time, this person— due to the maturity of the organization—would have no team. He would have to do all of the hands-on implementation work himself. We wound up reaching out to more than 230 people on this search, more than double the number for a typical search. The reason? The director-level people didn't have the technical skills (or desire) to roll their sleeves up quite so high, and the technical people were not strategic enough. We did fill the role, but it took a long time.

As CIO, you want what you want when you want it, and a search firm's responsibility—once it agrees to an engagement—is to get it for you. But the more you match your requirements to the career paths that IT professionals actually follow, the faster you will fill your roles.

Plan carefully

During the last week of February 2010, I received a call from a CIO whose company had decided to launch a program to implement a global single instance of an Oracle ERP system on May 1. None of his senior leaders had Oracle experience, and he needed to hire a program manager with specific experience in Oracle right away. He figured that eight weeks would be enough time to recruit, hire, and onboard the new program leader, as long as we could begin showing him résumés "yesterday."

Think about it. If I am doing a CIO search and I call to recruit you, it may take us a week to connect. Once we have our initial conversation, you need to review the position description and, most likely, discuss it with your spouse, particularly if it involves relocation. You will want to sleep on it, and eventually you call me back. We still need to do our own round of interviews, and if you are involved in some kind of major project (which you almost always are) that will take some time. Multiply that by a short list of five candidates, and the recruiting process extends to a good five or six weeks before we can present a slate of candidates. Even if a company is extremely efficient in scheduling interviews (and most companies are not), the interview phase will take another month (especially since the candidates are probably on global projects themselves). Then there is the time it takes to make an offer, for the candidate to resign, and for the start date to arrive.

When you are a CIO, there will be days when one of your senior leaders announces her resignation and you have fires to battle. You need résumés yesterday, and it is a search firm's job to get them for you. (That's why you engage us in the first place.) But even if you are using the best IT recruiter in town, most searches will take longer than you think. Another recruiting paradox: *CIOs are probably better at strategic planning than any other executive, but they don't always apply that skill to their recruiting needs in order to launch a search before their world is on fire.*

Devote the time

You are busy, incredibly busy, and you're even busier than usual because you have some open positions on your senior leadership team. If you go to the trouble of hiring a search partner, give her some time up front and talk with her about the role. A position description gives some information, to be sure, but it hardly tells the whole story. Your recruiter has questions: How would you rank the top requirements for the role? How would you sell the opportunity to your favorite candidate? What is the culture of the team you already have in place? Investing the time at the beginning of the search to talk through the role with your recruiter will save you a lot of pain and anguish down the road. Your recruiter has documents she needs you to approve—the final position description, the target company search list. The longer you take to approve those documents, the longer your search will take. If you don't have the time, appoint a trusted direct report who can act on your behalf.

The Interview Phase

What is simpler than running an interview process? Gather your interview committee, schedule the interviews, assess the candidates, and select the winner. In many organizations the interview process is this simple, and the hiring manager enjoys nice, short, successful searches with great hires. But in others, the interview stage is where the recruiting process loses the most momentum.

Stay in touch

A few years ago, the CIO at a high-tech company asked my recruiting firm to fill a VP of application development position for her. Her internal recruiters had exhausted the local market, so she asked us to conduct a national search. She knew that the company was headquartered in an area where many people would not want to relocate, so we all acknowledged up front that if we found a "live one" we would act quickly to move that candidate through the interview process.

We recruited for about three weeks and presented three strong candidates. I e-mailed the candidate materials to the CIO with a request for an appointment to review them by phone. I received a call from her assistant saying that the CIO would be in Singapore for the next three weeks and then India for the following two. She would be in back-to-back meetings during her trip and certainly not available to review our candidate materials or conduct interviews. Five weeks later, when the CIO returned, the candidates already had a bad feeling about the company, and our client lost her shot at them.

Much of that experience was my fault; I should have asked whether there would be any major obstacles to the search and, if there were, requested that the CIO identify a proxy who could move things along in the meantime. That's what I do now. If your recruiter doesn't ask for a proxy, you might consider assigning one, anyway.

Keep the first round small

A key mantra that I hear CIOs use when discussing processes or infrastructure or development is "Keep it simple." I would say that the same goes for the interview process. When a recruiter presents you with six candidates, you will want to interview all of them before narrowing the pool to two or three.

Hiring managers sometimes make the mistake of including way too many people in that first round. And it's no wonder. Your new head of solutions delivery will need to work well with the senior leaders on your team as well as your business partners across the company. But those interviews can take weeks to set up and will push your candidate's start date back by alot. Despite the fact that your recruiting partners have vetted these candidates, you still might decide in the first fifteen minutes that one of the candidates looks at you funny and you do not want him on your team. And yet that person is scheduled to meet your VP of sales for lunch. A much better process is to set up a short first round with just you and an HR leader and leave the rest of the interview team for your two finalists.

Prep the hiring committee

Candidate interviews are tricky. They are part skills evaluation, part relationship building, and part selling the company and the role. I have had candidates tell me, "Each person I met with had a different perception of this position. I don't think they really know what they want." Or, "The interview was fine, but there is nothing really compelling about the company or the role." Then there was the time (I kid you not) when a candidate reported that the interviewer fell asleep during the meeting. The candidate had to clear his throat to wake the guy up, and the interview continued.

Once you get to the final set of interviews, you and your interview committee are auditioning too. Most likely, your favorite candidate will receive a counteroffer from her current employer or is interviewing at other companies. You and your team have to conduct an impressive interview. Sit down with your team before the interview to make sure you are all on the same page about the role. Remind them that their job is to sell the company and the position as well as to evaluate candidates.

The Offer Stage

The offer stage is a thrilling but scary time for recruiters. We have identified and presented a strong candidate, kept her engaged and excited during the interview phase, checked her references, evaluated her compensation, and kept a handle on the other employment opportunities she is considering. But what we cannot do is ensure her acceptance of your offer. We can ask her if she'll accept the offer, and weigh her genuine interest in the role, but if her company makes a counteroffer or another employer moves more quickly than our client, we all may lose out after all that hard work.

Remember that time kills deals

Joe and Larry and Sue and Kate, all members of your interview team, still have to give you feedback on your two finalists, but they're involved in a major project, and then Larry goes on vacation. The candidates will just have to wait a few more weeks. Can your recruiter keep them warm? Or, you and your team have decided that John is the candidate you would like to hire, but you have to put his offer request through your finance committee, and you have this board meeting coming up, so it will be a few more weeks.

At the beginning of a search, the hiring manager is desperate to hire a new person for the position as quickly as possible. But at critical moments throughout the search, the company engages in a protracted decision-making process that at best causes major delays and at worst causes the company to lose its best candidate to a competing offer.

Give your interview team deadlines for delivering feedback, and stay on top of HR during the offer process. The faster you can deliver an offer, the sooner you can hire your winning candidate.

Keep your recruiter close

Your recruiting firm's job as your search partner is to build a relationship of trust with the candidates they present. The recruiter will have spent hours with the candidates discussing their hopes and dreams and talking through why this new job is good for them and their families. The recruiter will have discerned how important a role compensation plays in the candidates' assessment of the position, and what elements of a compensation package will work for them.

Most companies conducting searches know this and involve the recruiter in the offer stage. But every once in a while, a hiring manager and his HR partner, particularly those who are not used to working with external search partners, decide to "take it from here" when it comes to determining the final offer. They come up with the offer themselves, call the candidate to give her the numbers, and then the candidate calls the recruiter when the offer does not align with her expectations. The recruiter winds up in reaction mode, which is never good for anyone. Personally, I am always delighted when the hiring manager wants to make the actual offer himself. I believe it is an important part of building a relationship that we all hope will last for many years. But allow your recruiter full participation in the formation of that offer. It is part of what you are hiring them to do.

Beware the dark period

There is a part of the search that we at Heller Search call "the dark period." The dark period can occur at either of two specific points in the search. The first is when the finalist knows that she has been selected but, because of administrative issues, it is taking a while to produce the actual written offer. The second comes when the candidate has accepted the offer but is not due to begin work for another month. As recruiters it is our responsibility to keep your candidate warm and to serve her up no matter the circumstances. But one of the primary reasons the candidate wants the job is that she is going to work for you. She is excited about having you as her manager. When the going gets tough—and the offer is taking weeks—a call from you, the CIO, will go a long way toward sustaining your selected candidate through the dark period.

The Perfect Search

The CIO of a $15 billion company hired us to recruit a director of application development. As is the case with searches (and life), there were significant challenges to the search. (If there weren't, why would anyone ever hire a search firm?) The location was a challenge; the compensation had a nontraditional mix of a low base compensation and a high bonus, and the titling conventions of the company were such that VP-level candidates needed to be willing to accept a director title. But the role itself—running the development organization to support several specific lines of business—was not a purple squirrel. There was a bona fide talent pool available for the role.

The search was a great success. We began the search in mid-January, and the new director started work a mere ten weeks later. Here's why:

The CIO, let's call him "Joe," knew that the search could be challenging and hired us to launch it the day after the incumbent announced his resignation. He scheduled our kickoff meeting with him that same week. At our meeting, he gave us the PowerPoint presentation he had recently used to outline the company's IT strategy for the board. He spent more than ninety minutes with us and was generous with his answers to our many questions about the role, the company, and its culture. He also gave us access to other members of the executive committee so we could get a multidimensional view of the organization. After the meeting, Joe turned around approvals on the position description and the targeted search list the day we sent them. *He prioritized the search.*

Then, Joe did something wonderful. He let us recruit. He knew that it would take a several weeks for us to work our networks and surface the best candidates in the market (as opposed to the first we could lay our hands on) and was satisfied with our weekly e-mailed updates during the recruiting phase. Once we presented our slate of six candidates, Joe agreed to our recommendation that he do hour-long phone interviews with each of the six and narrow them down to four. He flew all four in for meetings with him and his VP of HR, and then brought the two finalists in for a final round to meet with a much more sizeable group. He prepped his interview team on exactly what they should be looking for in this role, and made sure that the finalists received a consistent message about the company and the position throughout their day of interviews.

Joe had his very competent administrative assistant handle all of the travel through the interview phase, and when Joe took a week of vacation in the middle of the search, his head of HR was able to move things along in his absence. As usual, there were considerable administrative tasks that needed to happen along the way, including travel arrangements and interview schedule confirmations. Joe's assistant handled everything expertly and the candidates went into their second round with the knowledge that Joe and his team were on top of their game.

At offer time, Joe took our advice on the elements of the offer and allowed us to secure a verbal acceptance from the candidate before he directed his HR organization to craft a formal offer. Once the candidate accepted, Joe called him the following week to touch base.

Conclusion

The perfect search doesn't sound all that tough to pull off, and many of our clients come very close to our experience with Joe. But many CIOs are so busy that the tasks required to run a good search often fall by the wayside. Don't get me wrong: in the end, this is the search firm's problem. When you hire a recruiter to find you qualified candidates, it is her job to put the pedal to the medal and complete the search despite the obstacles you throw in the way. But the more time your recruiter spends managing you, the less time she will spend in the talent market. Remember, we have a talent crisis on our hands, and you need recruiting to be a core competency. The devil is in the details, and if you go to the trouble of hiring a search partner, put the process in place to make the relationship a success.

8

The Enterprise Architecture Paradox

When a CIO tells me that she is going to need to hire an enterprise architecture leader, I have mixed feelings. On the one hand, I know that she'll need to work with a specialized IT executive recruiter; this means a new engagement for my firm, so I am happy. But when I think about the path ahead, about the process of getting on the same page with the CIO about what she wants in an enterprise architect, I am a little nervous. My team and I are excited for the challenge, and we know that—come hell or high water—we will be successful but, we also know the search will be tough.

Breaking Down the EA Paradox

Why? What is the problem with finding great enterprise architecture talent? Well, let's think about it. The winning candidate needs to have some sort of expertise in every layer of the technology stack, the ability to manage a matrixed pack of often entrenched and siloed technologists, a deep understanding of the business, and the interpersonal skills to sell concepts like service-oriented architecture to frustrated business executives who would like very much not to hear about IT. I call this the Enterprise Architecture Paradox: *Technology genius meets business strategist meets accomplished manager meets expert communicator is a tall order, yet you need one in your organization.*

Depth versus flexibility

Lynden Tennison, CIO of $20B Union Pacific Corporation, agrees that the enterprise architecture function is paradoxical. "For those of us who have been in the technology field for any length of time, the holy grail is efficiency," says Tennison. "And the theorist in us believes, 'The fewer tools I have in my tool kit, the more cost effective I can be. If I can force standardization through an architecture model, I should inherently be able to drive efficiency.'" With a limited number of tools in place, the theory goes, you can train your people to go very deep into a certain set of technologies rather than having constantly to teach them something new. And with everyone really good at a small set of technologies, your IT organization is a veritable machine of technology production.

As with any great theoretical model, the proof is in the practice. "The paradox of that theory is that different problem domains do not fit so well into one ideal mega-model view of the world," says Tennison. "So you always find yourself fighting against these two competing interests. 'I want to drive efficiency, commonality, shared experiences, and deep learning in my staff but I need to be really responsive, quick to market, and able to take advantage of new technologies.' When you walk into the brain surgeon's office and you need a liver transplant, what do you do?"

Likewise, the businesses you support tend not to fit into one architectural model. "What's important to marketing isn't always important to finance," says Tennison. "There is certainly some commonality, but marketing may need innovative, high-touch products that are antithetical to what is important to finance: tight controls and a very limited set of options."

As is versus future state

Tom Feichtinger is vice president of enterprise architecture at Waste Management, and prior to that he led enterprise architecture organizations at Dana Holdings and GM. In his view, enterprise architects often spend far too much time inventorying where they are now, rather than thinking through where they are going. "If the enterprise architecture team spends all of their time collecting and understanding what applications, platforms, data, and business processes they have, the group will add little or no value early on," he says. "I remember a consultant once asking me 'Why would you care about capturing your entire *as is* state? You are not going to use 90 percent of it for years,' and then a little light bulb went on for me. I should spend more time thinking about where we are going, not where we are now."

If you are planning a trip to the South of France, you don't spend the majority of your planning time mapping out the restaurants in your hometown. Why do architects spend so much time on the current state? "Part of the problem is that technologists tend to think in a linear way. 'I start here, complete this phase, then move to the next, and then the next, and eventually, that process will lead me to where I'm going,'" says Feichtinger. "Even the visionaries think, 'I need to know the details of our current environment eventually, so I better just collect them now.'"

When Feichtinger was at GM, the company owned a satellite company whose networks GM used to communicate with its dealership networks. When the Internet came along, GM decided to stop using those satellite networks. "When we did our future state thinking around our communications systems, it would have been a waste of time to learn all of the hardware, software, protocols, and business processes of those satellite networks," says Feichtinger. "The details of that architecture became pretty useless when we decided not to use them anymore."

Theoretical versus practical

When we interview candidates for our enterprise architecture searches, one area we spend quite a bit of time exploring is their ability to balance theoretical architectural models and tools with delivery needs of projects on the ground. "If your architecture organization spends too much time creating esoteric or very conceptual single models of the world, it is easy for them to become disconnected from the people who are actually trying to build and implement solutions," says Union Pacific's Lynden Tennison.

"We ran into this paradox all the time at GM," says Feichtinger. "Some of us would be rolling up our sleeves and ensuring the projects were successful, and we used to make fun of the people who we wouldn't see for weeks as they worked on big PowerPoints about taxonomies and processes. They'd come back down from the ivory tower and we'd say 'We've changed all the standards while you were gone.'"

Strategic versus tactical

As dangerous as it is to leave your architects in the ivory tower, it is just as dangerous to yank them out of it too often. "Both at GM and at Dana, the CIO felt the urgency of immediate cost cutting pressures, and would ask enterprise architecture to focus on tactical projects like, 'Find me an extra $10 million in operational costs,'" says Feichtinger. "Some of your best people end up on your architecture team, so when big, meaty issues come up in projects, you want those people involved. So you keep pulling them away from doing that important strategic work." In other words, you may find the extra $10 million, which is great, but you never get to develop a vision and a strategy for mobile computing.

Think About How You Manage the Function

My team and I have interviewed hundreds of enterprise architecture leaders, and we see a disturbing pattern. These executives were brought in to build an enterprise architecture function, but because of the paradoxes we've just discussed, the company never really sees the business value of enterprise architecture and pulls the plug on the architecture function. Similar to what often happens with the CIO role, the executive committee is left with a sour taste in its mouth, and enterprise architecture gets a bad name. When a new CIO decides to hire an enterprise architect, the vicious cycle begins again.

Despite my ranting and raving (I am finding writing this chapter to be very cathartic!), many companies do build highly successful enterprise architecture organizations that provide clear business value. Here are some approaches they take to managing the function.

Be specific

CIOs who manage enterprise architecture functions are more apt to keep their groups focused on the future if they are specific about their goals. "If you ask your enterprise architects to tackle big questions, like 'What do you think about portals?' they'll come back with an inventory of the portal technology you have in place today," says Feichtinger. But if you tell your enterprise architecture head, 'I want you to define our strategy for customer-facing websites or portals or single sign-on for the enterprise,' you are pointing them toward the future and keeping them from inventorying your present-state.

Resist sending your architects off on tangents

Just as you, as CIO, have to walk the tightrope between the operational
and the strategic, so do your enterprise architects. Help them out by
resisting the urge to pull them into the weeds. Feichtinger recalls a time
at a previous company when his CIO pulled him away from developing a
customer portal strategy in order to develop a set of rules for determining where IT resources should be physically located. "The portal strategy was directly related to revenue, and the administrative task was not,"
says Feichtinger. "If you are constantly pulling your architects onto tactical projects, you may get a hundred little things done, but you'll never
get that long-term value."

But don't overlook the short term

At the same time, if your architects spend months at a time doing nothing but long-term planning, they will fail to deliver short-term value,
and will fall prey to the "What have you done for me lately?" syndrome.
One approach Feichtinger has used to balance the long-term planning
versus short-term value conundrum is to build a plan for every application. "By developing a plan for every application, you quickly save money
by identifying applications that you can consolidate and simply shut off,
while at the same time, you are setting the road map for the future," he
says. "Both at GM and Dana, and now in process at Waste Management,
we were able to have some short-term wins that turned into longer-term
strategic value."

Lose the "standards police" mentality

When CIOs tell me that their enterprise architecture organization is in
need of a talent upgrade, one of their most common complaints is that

the group has built a culture of standards enforcement that slows projects down and builds resentment among the development groups. Feichtinger recalls, earlier in his career, inheriting an enterprise architecture organization from a leader who graded technology projects on their compliance standards. "He would give projects grades of 40 percent or 50 percent and hold back development until the standards were met," says Feichtinger. "But the developers were working with leading-edge technologies, where there were no standards. The enterprise architecture group was holding back innovation, and nobody likes to get graded."

Feichtinger and his group did away with the grading process and decided instead to get out in front of those projects where there were no standards and to create them. Currently at Waste Management, "We are putting mobile devices in the trucks to improve our truck routing capabilities, but we didn't have a standard for how to communicate with those vehicles," says Feichtinger. "Waste Management IT could slow the project down by months while we develop the standards, but instead, we got out in front, evaluated the device, and figured out how we were going to do it. So when the development team was ready to start, the standards were already there."

Find the Right Talent

I've said it before, and I'll say it again: It is hard to find great enterprise architects in the market. They are out there, to be sure, but they are in high-demand and are cautious about their employment opportunities. "Are you *really* looking for an enterprise architect?" they wonder. "This role smells more like a solutions architect to me. Does the company *really* support a true enterprise architecture function or am I going to wind up losing my resources six months in?" While you will no doubt need to go outside for EA talent once in a while, you will be in a far better position if you can grow your own.

Look beyond technology skills

Lynden Tennison has a good track record of growing his enterprise architecture talent. He has been CIO of Union Pacific since 2005 and has never had to recruit an EA leader from the outside. "My personal bias is that it is better to grow enterprise architecture skills from within," he says. "I think it is very hard to hire these people; not impossible, just very hard."

If you are like most executives, your natural tendency might be to reward your best technologists with advancement, but Tennison suggests that when it comes to enterprise architecture, you go a different way. "In many organizations, the enterprise architect role is given to the lead technologist; the title is the prize that goes to the person who is deepest in a particular field. 'He's my best Java programmer, so I'll make him my architect,'" Tennison says. "The problem with that approach is that your enterprise architect needs to get out of a single model and be able to move from one technology to another, to be able to transition as the stack needs to transition." And so we arrive at yet another tenet of the Enterprise Architecture Paradox: *You need to hire the right talent now to be prepared for a future you cannot see.* "If you knew what 80 percent of your framework would look like down the road, you could pick the people smartest about that framework and have them build and enforce the standards," Tennison says. "But what do you do when your marketing organization shows up and says, 'Gosh, the web was great, but we're ready for mobile'?" In that scenario, your Java programmer would be out of his element, and you would have to replace your enterprise architect.

Annabelle Bexiga, CIO of TIAA-CREF, agrees that one key to staffing your enterprise architecture function is avoiding the temptation to promote your strongest technologist into the role; soft skills, she believes, are an important part of the equation. As an architect, "you have to insert yourself without inserting yourself," she says. "Application developers do not like to build something because someone told them to do it." So, you need an architect who has the technical skills to set the standards, but a small enough ego that he can be diplomatic in enforcing those standards." In other words, architecture is as much about being inclusive as it is about understanding technology. "When you are promoting someone into an architecture leadership role, you are looking for diplomacy as much as technology," says Bexiga.

Make it formal and commit the time

At Union Pacific, Tennison has a rigorous process for grooming technical talent for more senior roles. It starts with an annual organizational review during which Tennison analyzes his entire 1,800-person IT organization to identify gaps in bench strength, high performers, and advancement opportunities. "We spend a couple of days locked in off-site meetings going through the whole organization, layer by layer," he says. As part of that process, Tennison and his HR IT director have a formal review with every director (one layer down from his executive team) and conduct a thorough evaluation of his or her entire staff. "We ask them, 'What kind of attrition do you see in the future? What is your mix of contractors to employees? What are the gaps you have in critical skills?'"

Tennison spends the most time in these meetings talking through all of the high performers. "While we are always on the lookout for management potential, we are also eager to identify people with the technical skills to develop into architects," he says. "I have to tell you, these meetings eat up my calendar. There are days when I come to work and I see three of these meetings on my calendar, and I think 'I just can't get out of these things!' But this is how I build my organization, so I don't let it slide."

I know what you're thinking. Who *doesn't* have a formal organizational review process? Who *doesn't* have a disciplined approach to grooming their technical talent? How is this any different from what I am doing? The difference lies in the exceptional success of Tennison's program. He has a team of strong enterprise architects, and he never goes outside for them. If the sheer volume of calls my firm receives from CIOs asking us to recruit their next architect is a sign, the results of Tennison's IT career development program are an anomaly. (I realize that if you take this advice and start to grow your own architects, my firm will lose a major revenue stream, but since my destiny is to be a Broadway star, anyway it is high time I got out of the recruiting game…)

Get 'em while they're fresh

About ten years ago, before Tennison had put in his talent development program, Union Pacific was transitioning to some new technologies and wanted to ramp up quickly. Tennison hired some experienced developers from the outside. He found that while the new hires were smart and had some great technical skills, they had such different approaches to technology frameworks that they could not work together productively. "They spent a lot of time arguing about approaches when any one of the solutions would have been okay," says Tennison. "They were debating whether they needed a Ford or a Chevy, and I'm thinking 'Who cares? Just pick one. They both get me down the street.'"

As an antidote to this problem, which amounted to a cultural issue, Tennison decided to do more than 80 percent of his hiring from the pool of recent college graduates. "This way, new hires learn how we do business, and that drives consistency and productivity," says Tennison. That doesn't mean that he isn't open to new ideas, but "we do set the expectation that there is an overarching strategy and architecture that we are working within."

Resist the urge to put them to work too quickly

To reiterate a theme from the last two chapters, a little patience goes a long way when it comes to running IT, whether you are keeping the business at bay as you set up shared accountability, recruiting from the outside, or training newly hired technology talent.

Once Tennison's college recruits are on board, they go through twelve weeks of training. "We start with teaching them how the business works," says Tennison. "How does a railroad work? What does marketing do? How does finance work? We take them out into the field and show them a rail yard, some of the things that the other businesses don't care about, but that are important to us." Next up is their IT training. "We take them through our standards. How do you do software changes? How do you do configuration management and bug reporting. How does our ticketing system work?" And as the capstone to the training, each new hire is given a project to work on, which she then presents to the management team in her area.

While a three-month training program for college hires seems sensible enough, not everyone in Union Pacific's IT organization agrees. "Every manager hates the program, because they want their new hire now," says Tennison. "They have projects that they need to get done, and they do not believe they can wait three months for this person to hit the ground. But we tell them they have to be patient."

Go it alone

Kumud Kalia, CIO of Akamai Technologies, has a different take on the Enterprise Architecture Paradox. "I don't think that companies are set up to put the enterprise architect at a level where they can make real contributions," he says. "Look at the skills and attributes of what an enterprise architecture position requires. Those skills and attributes are nearly identical to what is required of a CIO."

I remember doing a search for a chief architect for a financial services company. The requirements were that the person be a business strategist, relationship builder, change agent, outstanding manager, and superior technologist. I turned to my director of recruiting and said, "It seems like what we are really recruiting is a CIO." In the end, the chief architect we recruited was a former CIO who was happy to get on the CIO succession plan of a larger company. But that's an anomaly. Most CIOs are not willing to move into an architecture role.

"When you are recruiting an enterprise architect, are you actually recruiting what amounts to another CIO but with no staff or operational responsibility?" asks Kalia. "Who really wants that job?" The Enterprise Architecture Paradox to which Kalia alludes: *The best candidates to lead enterprise architecture often do not want the job.* Or, they do want the job, and they take it, but not for long. "I've been fortunate enough to find people who are good enterprise architects, but then they get picked off to do CTO or CIO jobs," says Kalia. "In the end, they want to run their own show."

Kalia's answer to this element of the Enterprise Architecture Paradox is temporarily to do away with the function. "I do not currently have a head for enterprise architecture," he says. "I assign enterprise architecture responsibilities to other members of my core team." Kalia has "mini-CIOs" over the company's lines of business, and it is up to them to define the architecture for their own area. "In this model, the notion of an enterprise architecture leader who spans the entire company goes away," says Kalia. Who is looking after the overarching enterprise architecture? "That's my job," says Kalia, "Until I find my next head of enterprise architecture!"

Conclusion

In 2011, I wrote a column for *CIO* magazine on the topic of enterprise architecture, and I received a ton of feedback. People e-mailed me that they have been struggling with enterprise architecture for years and have not yet gotten it right. I met people at conferences who told me that the column spoke directly to the challenges they had long been having with the enterprise architecture function. And I know from the number of enterprise architecture positions that we have filled over the years, CIOs have a tough time growing the right leader in-house.

In many ways, the enterprise architecture position embodies much of the CIO Paradox: be technical and strategic, but also practical and innovative; be incredibly smart but have no ego. And with all that going for you, you still have to want the job.

The Enterprise Architecture Paradox is a tough one, never more so than today when cloud and data and services and mobility are really shaking up the stack. Still, there are steps you can take to mitigate the challenge:

- *Grow your own.* Keep an eagle-eye on your IT ranks and always be on the lookout for those beautifully blended technology executives. When you find one, develop her, but don't mistake technical talent for EA talent.
- *Make them as senior as you can.* When EA leadership roles report to the CIO, the search is more successful and the talent is better. EA leaders are wary of reporting too low in the organization where they will not have the vantage point or visibility to do their work. If you push EA leadership down too many rungs, you will wind up with solution architects, not strategists or visionaries.
- *Balance their work.* Focus your enterprise architecture too far into the future, and they will wind up lost in academics and theories. Bury their heads in projects, and you'll never have a roadmap. Like so much of the CIO's role, managing the EA function is a balancing act.

9

The Successor Paradox

I tend to ask CIOs a lot of questions. One of my favorites: If you were to win the lottery and leave the working world forever, do you have a successor who can step into your shoes tomorrow?

I typically get one of three answers. Of the CIOs I ask, 50 percent tell me, "I am grooming two people, but they still have some development ahead of them. They need to think more strategically and be better at executive level relationships." Another 30 percent say, "I have someone who could take over my job tomorrow." And the remaining 20 percent shuffle their feet and sheepishly answer, "Not by a long shot." (In fact, the vast majority of the VP searches my firm conducts for CIOs have "CIO successor qualities" as one of the criteria.)

Despite the fact that most CIOs know that it is their executive responsibility to name and develop a successor, a small percentage of Fortune 500 companies honor the CIO's succession plan. The vast majority get their new CIOs from the outside. Hence the paradox: *You develop successors, but the CEO almost always goes outside for the next CIO.*

The Challenges of CIO Succession

This paradox has one obvious explanation: the CEO is dissatisfied with IT and the CIO's would-be successors are guilty by association. As Kevin Hart, CTO and CIO of Cox Communications, puts it, "When the CEO or the board perceives that something with technology has gone horribly wrong, the technology organization—rightly or wrongly—suffers a negative halo effect. If the current leader couldn't get it right, the CEO may think, 'We need to change this up, search externally, and start over.'"

But there are other, almost structural, challenges at play in the succession-planning paradox. One is the stovepipe dilemma, where IT leaders tend to come up through either infrastructure or applications. The CIO role requires experience with both, and CEOs are not willing to take a chance on a first-timer. Another is the exposure dilemma, where the executive committee has had too little interaction with the internal candidate to accept him as a C-level executive. Interestingly, many CIOs also report a desire dilemma, where not every direct report wants the anguish and accountability of the CIO position.

For Barbra Cooper, who recently retired as CIO of Toyota Motor North America, there is an additional explanation. With CEOs and other business executives still struggling (believe it or not) to gain a clear understanding of the CIO role, "They identify and define the role by the qualities of the person who is in it at the time," says Cooper. If the outgoing CIO is beloved, the executive committee, with no other measures by which to evaluate candidates, looks to replicate the incumbent's personality. And because personalities are unique and complex and not truly replicable, members of the executive committee cannot possibly be satisfied with any of the internal candidates in front of them. "Much of what my executive peers have responded to has been my personality," says Cooper. "So, about six years ago, when I started to put names on my succession list, the executives looked at me and said, 'What? Are you kidding? Those executives don't fit the role at all. We'll need to go outside and find another you.'" In many companies, the search for that perfect replica is never successful, and the revolving CIO door starts spinning.

A related reason for the relative scarcity of internal promotions to the CIO role has to do with the fact that technology changes so rapidly. As a result, IT's impact on the business is always changing, and each new generation of CIOs is likely to be quite different in skill set, approach, and even personality than the previous one. Barbra Cooper has been leading IT for more than thirty-five years. She has held executive IT positions at Miller & Paine department stores, American Express, Maricopa County in Arizona, and MicroAge. She joined Toyota's IT organization as a vice president in 1996 and has been there ever since. Cooper describes her own generation of CIOs as "legacy, in that we tend to be introverted, technically savvy, operationally strong, and command and control oriented."

But with the role of technology and the IT organization changing so dramatically every decade, Toyota's next CIO needs an entirely different leadership style and skill set than Cooper. This is a critical point often missed by both the executive hiring committee, which is still looking for that traditional model, and the current CIO, who may be tempted to model her successor in her own image.

So, the decks are stacked against a CIO's ability to develop a succession plan that the executive committee accepts and embraces. As CIO, your choice is just to run IT and let the CEO worry about how to fill the role when you leave or figure out a way to develop great successors—whether they succeed you at your company or move on to bring inspired IT leadership to another.

Assuming that you are a decent and responsible executive, and you opt for the second path, let's discuss ways you can develop future CIOs.

Identify a Successor for Tomorrow, Not for Today

As CIO, you have to be out in front of the company, envisioning the future of your industry, your business, the technology marketplace, and the way that your company and customers will make effective use of technology. Add "future CIO" to that mixture and stir. What are the qualities that the next CIO of your company will need to possess? The skill set and personal attributes of the executive who runs IT in the future will most likely be much different from your own. "If you're planning to retire in the next few years and your replacement is another 'you', someone who has worked under you for the past thirty years and has adopted your approach and vision, it is probably a huge miss," says Cooper.

With this, we have another tenet of the CIO successor paradox: *You need to maintain a staff that has the skills of the past, who can work on legacy systems and keep everything running as it should. But you also need to develop talent that can lead in the future.* And with the pace of technology change, you can only hazard a guess at what skills that talent will need to bring to the table. And it's not like once you identify those skills, you can go to the deli counter and order two-thirds of a pound of relationship building and a quarter of a pound of mobile strategy expertise. You need to develop these leaders.

Train your fellow executives

"The lines between business and IT roles are blurring," says Cooper. "If you cannot articulate how technology will impact the next ten years of your business and the kind of IT leadership the company is going to need, then you cannot present an effective successor. Unless you've readied the business for a new leadership style—based on your predictions about technology—they won't accept the successor you've been grooming, and you're stuck."

This is more easily said than done. Many CIOs cannot get the business to respect and value the current IT organization, let alone set a vision for the future of IT and for the ideal set of attributes of the next CIO. But if you have good relationships with the business, you can use that platform to pave the way for your successor. "I've always felt that in the last five years of your career, 40 percent of your efforts should be spent readying the business for the next generation of IT leadership talent," says Cooper.

Know your own career path

Before you define a path for your direct reports, you need to understand your own path, says Cox Communications' Kevin Hart. "The first question you have to ask is what you want for yourself," he says. "Do you want to be in this role for the next twenty years? Do you want to be promoted to COO? Do you want to pursue an external opportunity?" If you are not comfortable with your own next step, you will have a hard time defining the future for your successors. "Not everyone spends enough time thinking through their own career plans," says Hart. "That may hold them back from knowing how to invest in and mentor their team."

Start now

For CIOs who have thought through their own future, particularly if it means retirement in the next five years or so, it is time to set your sights on your successor. Your first order of business: don't assume that the candidate you have in mind is a shoe-in; test your assumptions. "Once you've zeroed in on your successor, you have to ensure that he or she will be accepted by the business community," says Cooper. "You have to make a conscious effort to be that person's agent, and put feelers out to your informal network to gauge their reaction." Once you've gotten some feedback on how this person is perceived by a wide range of business leaders, "you need to do an inventory of where the gaps are in terms of this person's ability to be accepted," Cooper says. And then you need to decide how you will close those gaps or whether there are just too many. "Either way, you do not want to be blindsided by the fact that the power players in the business are not accepting your direction."

Once you've managed to create a compelling vision for the future of IT and the skills your successor will require, you still need time to develop those skills in the successor you've identified. "New competencies are not something you can go out and pick off a tree like an apple," Cooper says. "You need to be able to observe that person over a period of time, to see how he can adapt to change."

Create mini-CIO roles

In all but a few of the CIO searches my firm conducts, the CEO privileges a sitting CIO over an up-and-comer. The CEO's typical attitude: "Let them get their CIO experience on someone else's dime. I need someone with scars on their back." The CEO's concern is that a candidate who has been in the number-two position will only have had applications leadership experience and will not be adept at managing the other 80 percent of the budget. Or he worries that the number two has only had operations experience and is not well versed in leading the front lines of IT, in facing off with the business and presenting them with innovative solutions. Or, possibly most worrisome to CEOs: the number two will not know how to manage the IT budget or handle herself in front of the board. Where we have been very successful in placing number twos into their first bonafide CIO position is by recruiting from the ranks of divisional CIOs. Here, while they still receive support and direction from a global or corporate CIO, they have led the panorama of IT functions and, ideally, have reported on their division to the board.

At Toyota, Cooper has built the concept of the mini-CIO into her leadership development plan. "In my IT organization, we had the front end of the business, application development, and the back end, operations and infrastructure, and the two were often very different cultures and had created their own silos," says Cooper. "Until I found a way to change the accountability model, I could never really test my leadership talent."

So, Cooper created a senior divisional level CIO role over, say, the Lexus division, where the mini-CIO and would own all of IT for that business. "These CIOs could not come back and blame everything on operations," she says. "By putting in the divisional CIO model, I could evaluate my potential successor's ability to handle end-to-end accountability."

Build a rotational program

About four years ago, Cooper determined that it was critical to the development of her potential successors that they serve time in non-IT leadership positions. So, she was frustrated by the fact that Toyota did not have a structured rotational program between the business and IT. She was finding that getting the business to value the concept of an IT person among their ranks was tough. "The business was still struggling with the definition of the IT leadership role and would ask 'Why would I take on an IT person? I don't know what I would do with them.'" Cooper says.

So Cooper first selected the managers she felt had the most potential to benefit from a rotational program. She then identified the business areas she believed could benefit from that IT talent, and she approached her business peers. "I actually drafted a written eighteen-month contract between two officers of the company, one on the business side, and me, the CIO, which outlined the terms and conditions of the rotational assignment," she says. The contract covered questions that included: What are the expectations of the role and the manager? What will the business's return on this investment be? Who is responsible for performance reviews? What happens at the end of eighteen months if the business doesn't want to give the IT executives back?

Not only was Cooper's rotational program a success in IT, it became a companywide program that provided rotational opportunities for high-potential employees across the enterprise.

Build a CIO University

Kevin Hart, CTO and CIO of Cox Communications, has developed his share of CTOs and CIOs. "I've been in the CIO or CTO role for seven years now," says Hart, "In that time I've been fortunate to have groomed more than ten CIOs. The majority has gone on to greener pastures to fill a CIO role at another company, but I did groom a successor who replaced me when I left a company to pursue a new opportunity."

Hart's first CIO role was in 2005 at Level 3 Communications, and he continued there until 2009, when he left to join startup Clearwire as CIO. In April 2011, Hart joined Cox Communications as CTO and CIO.

When Hart became CIO for the first time, at Level 3, he discovered what so many CIOs find during their first few months on the job. "I recognized that the leadership, confidence, and the mental model that we needed in the IT organization needed to be developed," he says. "The culture was more of IT as an order taker, which was pretty different from the culture I wanted to create, which was a mind-set of leaders, trying to bring technology and the business together." Hart realized that he needed to teach a whole different set of skills to his team, but he did not have the money to outsource the effort. "We were already strapped for budget to deliver our projects," he says. "I knew that there wouldn't be a whole lot of tolerance for spending ten or twenty grand per person to send them to a week-long program."

So Hart developed plans for what he calls "The CIO University," a year-long internal leadership development program that became so successful at Level 3 that he brought it to Clearwire and is now launching it at Cox. "We couldn't just swap out certain people and replace them with leaders overnight," says Hart. "So I decided to build a program to instill new skills into our leaders in a collaborative experience that we could apply day in and day out."

Here's how he did it.

Define the competencies

Kevin Hart's first move was to identify the areas of competency that he wanted the program to focus on, and he put together a core curriculum. The curriculum looked like this:

- DiSC profiles: DiSC is a personal assessment tool used to improve work productivity, teamwork, and communication
- *The Five Dysfunctions of a Team,* Patrick Lencioni (Jossey-Bass, 2002)
- Leadership Pipeline
- Stakeholder Management
- Thomas-Kilmann—*Practical Tools for Reducing Conflict: The Thomas-Kilmann Conflict Mode Instrument (TKI)*
- 7 Survival Skills
- Employee Engagement Improvement
- Managerial Effectiveness
- Communications
- Walking in our Customers' Shoes
- Organizational Values
- Technology Best Practices
- Leadership Lessons Learned (guest speakers include CEOs, CFOs, COOs, from the company)

Think about the classroom environment

Hart then chose the setting for the program. "We would go to the University of Denver or Colorado and rent a low-cost classroom every quarter that overlooked the football field," he says. "I thought it was important to have the participants be back on campus and have a university experience."

Balance classroom instruction with small group projects

Hart brought in outside experts in each of the competency areas to lead the entire class of thirty people. Those experts would then break the group into teams of five and give them an assignment to complete in the time between the quarterly classroom sessions. This required them to work together to take what they learned in the classroom and apply it in a real-world, workplace context.

"For example, we were good at high-level communication across the IT organization, but we had difficulty with communications between the manager level and individual contributor," says Hart. "Our managers were not translating projects and plans into specific action items."

To improve the team's one-on-one communication skills, a CIO University instructor assigned one of the groups the task of creating a manager's communication checklist. The document that the team produced included reminders, tips, and best practices for conducting one-on-one conversations and for using key performance indicators in performance evaluations. "It was a specific homework assignment that the CIO University class used to create a solution and roll it out across the entire organization," says Hart. "Then we'd come back the next quarter to have another all-day session on a new topic. But we'd also revisit the previous topic by having the team members report on what they put in motion, the results, and areas for improvement."

This program of full-day sessions coupled with on-the-job small team projects would continue for an entire calendar year. "Not only were they building on their own individual skills but they were collectively working to improve the entire IT organization," says Hart. "The CIO University became part of the transformational fabric of the culture of IT."

And Hart has proof. "When I first got to Clearwire, we had some of the lower satisfaction scores in the company; we were somewhere in the fiftieth percentile," he says. "A year after our first CIO University, we jumped nineteen percentage points to the highest employee satisfaction score in the company."

Hart enrolled thirty leaders in the company each year, held a graduation ceremony, and then invited the next thirty to join. "It got to the point where everyone wanted to go through the program," says Hart. "It became a self-fulfilling prophecy, where people got excited about becoming better leaders." In the end, Hart sent hundreds of people through the program at Level 3 and at Clearwire.

Keep it cheap

As for budget, Hart found ways to keep expenses down. "We would rent a room at a university, which was relatively low cost. We'd bring lunch in, and then I'd take everybody out to the campus pub," says Hart. "I got deals on the outside expert presentations by calling in favors from friends who were experts in certain fields. We would also bring in executives from other parts of the company." Including executives from other parts of the company had additional relationship benefits. "That was the secret sauce of the program," he says. "I had Jim Crowe, CEO of Level 3, come in and address the class on what he had learned about leadership over the last twenty-five years. Jim is a brilliant orator," Hart says. "That was probably the best presentation in three or four years."

Not only would the CEO, CFO, and other executives give great presentations free of charge, "it created a great bond between my team and our major stakeholders," says Hart. "The senior executives got to see what we were doing and gain a little more respect for what the technology team has to face day in and day out."

Emphasize humility

As successful as the CIO University has been, there is one thing that Hart might have done differently. "Going in, the team had pretty low morale; they weren't respected by their peers and didn't have a voice in the company," Hart says. "We changed that mind-set almost to the point where some of the team members got a little overconfident at times. In many respects, they knew more about the business than many business leaders, and they started to become overconfident at times when bringing new ideas to the table."

And now we come to yet another CIO Paradox: *To be successful, your team has to know more about the business than most of their stakeholders, yet overconfidence can be their undoing, with stakeholders offended by what they perceive as arrogance.*

Having the confidence to know a lot about a lot and the humility to be careful when displaying that knowledge can be very challenging, particularly for up-and-comers. "I tell my leaders that, while we have a lot of value to add, people are experts in their field for a reason," Hart says. "You need to feel comfortable bringing ideas to the table, but you need to be careful about overstepping your boundaries."

Conclusion

So, how do you know when you've broken The CIO Successor Paradox? One clear indicator is that the successor you choose is sitting in your office after you retire or move on. But, considering the many forces against you in making that happen, we need another measure of success. "I just got a note from a graduate of the CIO University program," says Kevin Hart. "He just landed his first CIO job, at a fast-growing company. To this day, I am always amazed and blown away by the feedback from the CIO University participants. They tell me that the program was their most meaningful leadership development experience by far, and while that is flattering, I'm scratching my head because, well, I just kind of pulled it together."

You know you have broken The CIO Successor Paradox when you can claim a role in the development of the next CIO generation. Some takeaways:

- *Rotate your high potentials into the business:* One of the primary reasons CEOs decide against your named successor is that neither she, nor the executive team, have seen him in action. By all means, having your best senior leaders present to the board is one way to give them executive level exposure, but that exposure is short lived. A rotational program will let successors build the relationships (and the skills) to secure the top spot.

- *Don't stop with IT:* The executive rotational initiative that Barbra Cooper started in IT became a company-wide program. Not only does her rotational program bring tremendous value to the entire company, Cooper gains the credibility as an enterprise leader, which allows her to do so much more with IT. We have already discussed this earlier in the book, but I will reiterate it here: CIOs who have managed to succeed despite the many paradoxes of the role have something in common: they have initiated in IT a program or methodology—like strategic planning, project management, or, in this case, leadership development—that their peers decide to adopt for their own departments.

- *Do it yourself:* At Toyota Motor sales, Cooper simply leveraged her skills as an executive comfortable with negotiating multimillion-dollar contracts and created a contract for use with her fellow executives, and Kevin Hart has brought his CIO University with him from job to job. Neither Cooper nor Hart waited around for their company's organizational design experts to build the program for them, and neither should you. You can involve organizational design, and human resources, and anyone else, for that matter, but it is your succession plan and you need to make it happen.

Senior IT Leadership Journey Assessment

The CIO Executive Council has loaned me this quick and simple assessment to indicate the general leadership capability of your IT organization's senior leadership team (the CIO's direct reports and their direct reports). Before you run out and design your new leadership development program, take a moment to understand just what competencies you already have.

Check the box for each action only if it is *routinely and typically* true for a *large majority* of your senior IT leadership team. (The assessment can also be adapted to apply to an individual senior leader.)

Our senior leadership team…

SECTION A

- ☐ Apply deep expertise in enterprise technologies and systems in their day-to-day roles
- ☐ Understand and respond appropriately to needs and requests of business stakeholders
- ☐ Relate their work to business goals and strategies
- ☐ Communicate effectively with business counterparts
- ☐ Build and lead effective teams
- ☐ Develop leaders effectively among their own direct reports
- ☐ Collaborate effectively across organizational boundaries

boxes checked_____

SECTION B

- ☐ Apply deep expertise in cross-enterprise business processes in their day-to-day roles

- [ ] Cultivate strong relationships with senior business stakeholders
- [ ] Represent IT as a trusted partner on cross-functional committees, teams, etc.
- [ ] Effectively apply influence, negotiation and partnering skills with our vendors
- [ ] Exert effective influence on business peers (to consider alternatives, adopt approaches, etc.)
- [ ] Originate ideas for business processe innovation that drive significant value
- [ ] Create and present to colleagues and stakeholders compelling strategic visions about the business

boxes checked_____ × 2 = _____

SECTION C
- [ ] Apply deep business and vertical industry acumen appropriate to their position in their day-to-day roles
- [ ] Have been recruited or transferred successfully to non-IT business function roles (any number)
- [ ] Originate ideas for innovating the customer experience that drive significant value
- [ ] Effectively represent or stand in for the CIO in meetings with executive committee
- [ ] Originate ideas that have been game changers for the business (affecting the business model, go-to-market strategy, etc.)
- [ ] Have been recognized by our executive committee as strong contenders to succeed the current CIO (at least two)

boxes checked_____ × 3 = _____

Scoring: Add the number of checked boxes in each section and multiply the result by the multiply factor (1 for Section A, 2 for

Section B, and 3 for section C. Add the three section scores to determine your total score.

Scoring Analysis: The CIO Executive Council recommends in its "Future-State CIO Journey" concept (council.cio.com/futurestate) that to deliver maximum value and remain relevant, IT staff must elevate their leadership capability from one that is largely functional and internally oriented on systems to an enterprise orientation with expertise in process transformation, to, ultimately, a more externally oriented focus with expertise in the business and strategy.

0–7 = Function-oriented, internally-focused
systems experts

Your IT leadership team is largely focused internally on managing the IT function and the systems and services it provides to the user community. To do this well, they are applying the competencies of people and organization development, team leadership and systems expertise. This focus is most often associated with IT organizations that primarily have a service provider role in the business, Consistent, excellent execution of these actions earns IT and its leadership a reputation for credibility, which is essential to advancing IT's role to that of a strategic value driver and business game changer.

To get to the next level, your leadership team needs to develop and apply the competencies of strategic orientation, change leadership, collaboration & influence and results orientation. They need to focus their leadership enterprisewide vs. internal, and they need to cultivate strong process expertise.

8–23 = Transformational-oriented, enterprise-focused
process experts

Your IT leadership team is largely focused at the enterprise level, and have built strong process expertise that they apply in enabling transformation. They apply the competencies of strategic orientation, change leadership, collaboration and results orientation. Building on their service credibility, your team has cultivated and is consistently applying a collaborative approach to working with the business. This positions your IT organization to be a trusted IT partner. With this reputation, your IT leaders have the power of influence over their stakeholder partners and thus over business strategy.

To get to the next level, your leadership team must focus more attention on, and apply expertise toward, the external drivers of the business. They should cultivate market knowledge, internalize the needs of external customers and develop a commercial orientation to spot market or customer service opportunities.

24–39 = Strategically-oriented, externally-focuses business experts

Your IT leadership team has developed and is applying expertise in the business itself, leveraging its external focus on customers, competition and markets to drive business strategy. Your team is no longer seen as just go-to collaborators for all things IT, or even as process gurus; they are largely accepted as true business peers who happen to have IT expertise. They are in a position to earn a game changer reputation for the IT organization. The most outstanding leaders in the group may have the background and competencies to succeed as future-state CIOs.

PART IV

Your Future: What's Next for the CIO?

10

The Corporate Board Paradox

I probably get more calls and e-mail from CIOs interested in sitting on corporate boards than I do on any other single topic. Despite evidence to the contrary, I am actually a nice person, and I like to be encouraging and give good news. But the fact is, very few corporate boards appoint CIOs. In fact, I was recently talking to an executive recruiter friend of mine (we recruiters do have friends, you know) who runs a practice focused exclusively on board placements. He told me that in his more than thirty years of recruiting board members, never once has he been asked to recruit a CIO.

This is a real paradox. We all know stories where a data security breach has wrought havoc on a company. We've seen as many situations where an IT innovation has given a moribund company a new lease on life. How can it be that corporate boards fail to see the value of a CIO's perspective?

Doreen Wright is a rare example of a CIO who has sat on a number of corporate boards. And it is no wonder: Wright has an impressive back-ground that spans multiple industries and functional leadership roles. She graduated from the University of Pennsylvania and then began her career at Merrill Lynch, where she managed retail client service units. In 1984, she joined Bankers Trust Company as vice president, institutional trust and custody marketing.

Wright was in her mid-thirties and managing director of trust operations at Bankers Trust during a time when the IT organization was implementing a $50 million trust accounting system. The systems leader became ill and had to leave. So, after the successful resolution of a major battle over funding for the project, the company had no one to lead it. Though she lacked real technology experience, Wright went to the vice chairman of the bank and said, "I can do this." The vice chairman was skeptical, but Wright told him that she could figure it out, and she was awarded the project. She wound up trading in her operations management career path for senior IT leadership roles at Bankers Trust, Prudential Insurance, and Nabisco, her first CIO role.

Wright was CIO at Nabisco from 1999 to 2001, and then CIO at Campbell Soup Company from 2001 until her retirement in 2008. In 2002, along with her role as CIO, Wright also served as Campbell's chief human resources officer. She has that beautifully blended profile that began in business and moved over to IT at an executive level, including two stints as CIO of large global companies, holding a concurrent role as head of HR at one of them. No wonder she is attractive to corporate boards.

Currently a member of the board of directors of the Dean Foods Company, the largest processor of milk and other dairy products in the United States, Wright also sits on the board of Crocs, the extremely popular footwear maker, and she is on several nonprofit boards, including New Hope Arts, Inc., a regional visual performing and literary arts center, and until recently, the Emerson College Communications Advisory Council. Previously, Wright was on the board of Citadel Broadcasting Corporation, the largest pure play radio company, Conseco, Inc. (CNO Financial Group), The Oriental Trading Company, The Yankee Candle Company, the Annenberg Center for the Performing Arts, and the American Repertory Ballet.

The Bias Against CIOs on Boards

With all that experience, Wright is in a good position to help us with our quandary: Why don't more boards appoint CIOs?

Generational bias

With the pace of technology change at an all-time high, and with 20-something CEOs making billions of dollars on technology start-ups, we forget that boardrooms are still populated by executives in their mid-sixties. "During their tenure as corporate executives, these people had an arm's length to IT," says Wright. "Many experienced IT as a necessary evil during a time when the business would throw the order over the wall to IT. Board members still have this very dated and inaccurate view of the CIO being too technical, not having good communication skills, and not being able to talk in business terms. That's a really old perspective, but because of the age of the sitting board members, that's what they remember, and those biases die hard."

Bad experiences

CIOs eager to sit on corporate boards also suffer from this CIO Paradox: *Your many successes are invisible, but your few mistakes are highly visible.* "Many board members have had a bad experience with IT," says Wright. "An ERP project didn't go well or they didn't see the benefits of a particular IT investment. Regardless of all the good IT did for them, they have had at least one bad experience, and they just can't let go of it. They are predisposed not to like CIOs, and they won't even entertain putting them on a board."

Preference for P&L leaders

Believe it or not, CIOs are not the only victims of corporate board bias. "If you look at Fortune 250 boards, you see that not only are there very few CIOs, there are very few functional leaders of any kind," says Wright. "Boards have to have a CFO, because they need a financial expert to lead the audit committee, but beyond that, boards will be heavy on CEOs and heads of business lines and light on functional leaders."

The inner circle

Some 50 percent of board appointments are handled through search firms, Wright estimates, with the other 50 percent occurring through referrals. "And don't let anybody kid you; it's still an old boy's network," she says. As CIO, if you are not well connected to a network of CEOs, CFOs, and P&L leaders, you will have a tough time breaking in.

Like Doreen Wright, Bob DeRodes broke in. Also like Wright, DeRodes started out in banking, where he assumed leadership roles in both technology and bank operations. But his career went in the opposite direction of Wright's. Whereas Wright started out as a banker and picked up IT as an executive, DeRodes started out in technology and used that experience to move into banking. Either way, the result is the same. CIOs who have traversed the fiery pit between the business and IT at least once in their careers—they have run non-IT operations or have run IT as a P&L—will have a much wider array of opportunities from which to choose, be it board work, COO roles, or general manager positions.

DeRodes earned a Bachelor of Science in Business Administration degree from Saint Louis University and an MBA from the University of Texas at Austin. For the first two decades of his career, he held technology roles at banks, including Society National Bank Cleveland, First National Bank in St. Louis, and USAA Federal Savings Bank. A respected executive who, like most CIOs, knew a thing or two about his company's operations, DeRodes was hired by USAA to open the first Federal Savings Bank in the country, becoming the SVP of bank operations. Later, he moved back into IT with USAA taking a senior corporate IT role. From there, he joined American Airlines to help form The Sabre Group, later becoming president of development services for the newly formed company, and then went back into banking as CTO for global card products at Citibank.

Next, DeRodes joined Delta Airlines as CEO of Delta Technology, a technology services company that provided IT services to Delta and other airline customers. In 2002, he moved into a new industry altogether, becoming CIO of The Home Depot.

This, by the way, brings us to another critical point about CIOs joining boards. The greater the number of industries in which you have played leadership roles, the wider your networks and your perspective, and the more valuable you will be to a board. Wright's industry involvement ranged from banking to consumer packaged goods. The industries in which DeRodes worked ran the gamut from banking to airlines to retail; in 2008, he went back to financial services, this time at First Data, again as head of technology and operations, reporting to the CEO.

At present, DeRodes leads DeRodes Enterprises, an IT and business operations consulting company and is on the board for NCR, the $5 billion technology provider to retail companies, and for Veracode, a privately held information security services provider.

Ignorance and discomfort

According to DeRodes, "CEOs recognize the importance of IT in their companies, but they often don't understand it. They are generally uncomfortable when dealing with technology, and they find the subject intimidating, frustrating, and incredibly boring. They understand that IT drives their factories and their supply chains and their marketing and their sales and service organizations; they understand that technology closes their books and enables their financial ecosystem, runs their capital markets, runs their communication networks, and even pays their employees. They understand all that," says DeRodes. "But for some reason, they don't seem to be able to connect the dots that IT holds the dubious honor of being the sole function that, if disabled or severely compromised, could literally put the corporation out of business."

CEOs are used to being the smartest people in the room. They typically have a healthy understanding of sales, finance, and business operations, having served as leaders over many of those functions. IT? Not so much. It takes an enlightened CEO to drag that subject matter into her board meetings.

Limited seats

Even for CEOs who are more comfortable with technology (and that number is, of course, increasing as the older generation of CEOs gives way to the new), CIOs just don't rank when compared with the other possibilities. "If I am limited to eight or twelve board seat selections, I could bring in another marketing executive, or a key customer I want to bring closer, or a government official who could help us in some way," says DeRodes. "So, why would I blow that seat on a CIO?"

The Case for CIO Board Appointments

At this point, you probably feel like you should just shut this book and take a moment to mourn the loss of a board experience during your career. But before you do that, and just to make us feel good, let's build the case for boards to appoint CIOs.

Diminishing supply of CEOs

With the economic volatility of the last several years, CEOs have to deal with problems at their own companies, and many no longer have the bandwidth to attend to another company's challenges. "The fact is, many companies do not want their own CEOs to sit on other boards. Board work is incredibly time consuming," says Doreen Wright. "In times of crisis, my own boards have met twenty times in a three-month period. These days, companies do not want their executives gone for that long."

Diversity of personalities is good

Boards often include a number of CEOs who have just retired and are not yet ready for a life of golfing and gardening. "There is a problem with this approach," says Wright. "These executives are fresh off of a successful CEO career, which is great, but now you have a board populated by people who are used to making all of the decisions. When you have too many chiefs around the table, it's a mess."

If you look at senior management teams as a model, you find a blend of CEOs, P&L leaders, and functional heads. "It is the functional leader, whether it is the CIO, head of HR, or head of legal, who understands how to do things in large enterprises in a consistent, cohesive manner," says Wright. "Functional leaders have to be highly collaborative. They have to understand how to reconcile big differences and natural tensions between, let's say, a P&L leader and a particular function. The functional leader has a very different orientation than a P&L leader, which can be very valuable for a board." And what works for an executive committee should work for a board.

CIOs have the broad view

My favorite phrase lately is: *The CIO is at the nexus of all things.* As CIO, there is no part of the business for which you do not have some sort of accountability. In such an integral role, you have an intimate knowledge of the business from beginning to end. "Boards need to understand that with a CIO, you are not just getting IT expertise," says Wright. "You are almost always getting more." The CIO is the only executive in the company who sees a business process from beginning to end. No other function, not even supply chain, sees everything: how you procure materials, how you make the product, how you package, ship, and sell it, how you collect the money in accounts receivable. So, just by definition, a CIO understands the company's business processes better than anyone. "That's an amazing perspective to have on the board," says Wright.

Crisis management

We can all cite scenarios where companies are in crisis precisely because of IT. A few years ago, my firm conducted a CIO search for a company whose $100 million, global, single-instance ERP implementation went horribly wrong. The project team missed most of its deadlines, the steering committee went back to the well for more funding a number of times, and the company's warehouses could not get up-to-date order information for weeks. In fact, things were so bad that the CEO said to me, "I know I won't get the benefits I wanted from the ERP system. My only hope now is that the project doesn't kill us." And that is nothing compared with companies that have experienced major breaches in customer information security. Wouldn't a board member with IT crisis management experience be of help here? "By turning a blind eye to IT, boards are ignoring one of the most key components of their chartered responsibility," says Bob DeRodes.

DeRodes cites the numerous service and information security failures of major corporations around the world. "One of the primary roles of a board is to govern over operational areas that can have a material impact on the corporations' financial condition or brand value. What single area inside the corporation has more opportunity to negatively impact these factors than IT? The risks associated with massive IT deployments are not only not well understood, but the backgrounds of the board members governing these companies rarely prepare them to ask the right questions of the CIO or, more importantly, understand the answers," he says.

Change management

Not only, as CIO, do you have intimate knowledge of the business, you also play a major leadership role in changing the business. "When we put in an ERP at Campbell, we changed 1,800 business processes," says Wright. "And I had to make sure that everyone was trained and everyone knew the new processes and everyone knew how to use the computer systems, and how to hold the hands of the people who were resistant to change." Most boards are leading their companies through some kind of transformation, and transformation falls squarely in the wheelhouse of the CIO.

Risk management is hot

Whenever there is an economic downturn or a major crisis, boards take a step back and reevaluate their membership. "Since 2008, more boards are conducting self-assessments and asking, 'Who do we have on the board? Let's check the boxes. We want to expand internally; do we have that expertise? What about our risk management challenges? Do we have that covered?'" says Wright.

According to Bob DeRodes, the evaluations that boards are currently conducting has led many of them to consider risk more closely. And, of course, CIOs have a unique perspective on the topic. "Boards would benefit from someone who can ask questions about how the IT organization identifies, categorizes, and manages risk, even at the highest level," he says. "Boards need someone who can say, 'Explain to me, CIO, how you categorize your risks, how you think about them, and then how you go about managing them. What are the execution plans behind that management?'"

Of course, boards have been talking about risk for years—it's a topic typically treated by board audit or finance committees. But risk has taken on a new meaning in our current technology environment. "Information security, privacy, compliance, all those issues are deeply embedded in the IT organization," says DeRodes. "As these issues get increasingly complex and high-tech, it is getting more difficult for even auditors to explain what we're doing and how we're doing it. So you're finding more and more board members wanting a technologist around the table just to be sure they understand what the IT organization is telling them about how they are protecting customer information."

Get Yourself On to a Board

The economic crisis of the last four years may actually have created an opportunity for CIOs to sit on boards: with risk on everybody's mind, with boards reevaluating their needs, and with CEOs—the most popular pool of candidates for board positions—in shorter supply, the time may well be ripe for CIOs to ascend to their rightful place at the boardroom table. So, just tear out these few pages, wave them in the face of your nearest board chair, and make your case about why you should be selected to serve. But before you do, let's talk about some other actions you should probably take to position yourself for board activity.

Leverage your own company's board

As an executive at Delta and Home Depot, DeRodes spent quite a bit of time with his companies' boards. "At Delta, I was the CEO of a subsidiary company, and at Home Depot, I was a member of the executive team, and our CEO wanted us to be at all of our board meetings. I found that the experience you gain from watching boards, their chemistry (or lack of chemistry), and how they operate is very valuable," he says.

DeRodes does acknowledge that there is a world of difference between presenting to your own board and sitting on a board as a director. "Going back in my career, I can remember a number of times I was summoned to the board," he says. "I was whisked in, nervous as hell. Then I'd try to give the best pitch of my life, and get whisked out again."

The real opportunity is in demonstrating to the board that you are that rare breed of leader with a perfect blend of business acumen, strategic thinking, technology expertise, and executive presence. "This is a chance to build your reputation as an individual who can be trusted with large decisions," says DeRodes. "It's a chance to show that you are a creative thinker who can identify and solve large problems, as opposed to somebody who worries about budgets and is a caretaker of an environment. Your chances of making the right impression on the board are diminished if you just come in and say 'Here's my budget and I'm hitting it.'"

Most board members are well connected and know which boards are looking for technology expertise. "If they can tell their networks, 'I know the CIO at the company where I'm on the board. He or she comes in and briefs us every quarter and is really impressive and knows the industry really well,' that would be a good starting point," says DeRodes.

While presenting to your own board is not a direct route to your first board appointment (and you're certainly not going to spend the whole meeting glad-handing and asking for referrals) building credibility and relationships among your own board members will position you well for board work.

Now may be a good time to ask yourself: How good am I at board presentations? Do I wow the board with my knowledge of the business and the impact that IT is having on its growth? If you are not truly capitalizing on the opportunity to impress this influential and captive audience, you might want to hire a coach and master the art of presenting to the board.

Target your vendors

As I mentioned earlier, boards often appoint executives from their biggest partner companies to strengthen an important relationship. Often, many large service organizations have a customer board, and participation there can also offer valuable board experience. "These customer boards have the ear of the CEO," says DeRodes. "I can tell you that at

HP and IBM, the CEOs pay close attention to those boards, and their lieutenants are in almost all of the meetings."

While customer boards play more of an advisory function than corporate boards, which play a governing function, they give you exposure to people outside your company. And if you can influence the product direction of one of your major vendors, that's a nice fringe benefit.

Pick up a new title

If a board of directors is going to appoint a CIO, they will be more likely to favor the candidate who has taken on more than IT. This is what I refer to as the "CIO-and phenomenon," where CIOs are adding SVP of customer care, chief human resources officer, or VP of strategic planning to their titles. Just as Doreen Wright was head of HR for Campbell Soup during part of her CIO tenure, a CIO who takes on more than IT demonstrates a broader set of leadership skills and changes those die-hard perceptions of CIOs as pure techies. "It's all about the diversity of your work portfolio," says Wright. "For a CIO to be asked to join a board, they need to be known for work that is broader than the CIO title." If you Googled Wright during her tenure at Campbell Soup, you would find interviews with her on workforce diversity and leadership development, in addition to articles about her in *CIO* magazine.

This, of course, puts me in mind of another paradox: As CIO, you need to grasp the big picture and the smallest detail, you need to manage a team of techies and teach them to "talk business," you need to balance cost containment and innovation, and you need an intimate view of every single process in your business. The job is hard and, it seems, beyond the grasp of most mere mortals. The Paradox? *As tough as the CIO role is, it is not enough simply to master it. If you want to move forward in your career, you should probably pick up another title as well.*

Join the right company

When Doreen Wright was at Campbell Soup, her CEO, Doug Conant, believed very strongly that each member of his executive team should sit on a board. "He knew that it would give his executives the ability to become better leaders and it would bring important knowledge back to Campbell Soup," says Wright. "By serving on boards, we learned new ways of doing things. We were getting an external perspective, which was invaluable. It also taught us how to be more effective with the Campbell Soup board. Serving on an external board immediately increased our credibility with our own board." If, unlike Doug Conant, your CEO sees no value in your joining a board and will not support your effort, either give up on the dream or give up on the company.

Build your executive search networks

"There are two ways that boards select their directors," says Wright. "Either they conduct a formal executive search, or they will act on a referral." Most large search firms have vertical practices (financial services, retail, industrial) and functional practices (CIOs, board practices, CFOs, heads of HR). When the CEO needs to recruit a new board member, she will approach the firm's board practice leader for the search. If the requirements include a heavy focus on technology, that board practice leader will go to the CIO practice leader and ask for names. If you don't already have a relationship with the CIO practice leaders at the major search firms, now would be a good time to start. "Two of my board appointments came to me this way," says Wright. "The company engaged a search firm and told them, 'We want a woman with a financial services background who has had experience with risk management and transformation.'" That recruiter walked right over to the head of the CIO practice and asked for suggestions. The CIO practice leader said, "Call Doreen."

The other route to board work is for the CEO to reach out to his own networks for suggestions. "At the end of the day, if your name isn't known among CEO or executive search networks, you are never going to make the list," says Wright. This is no different from anything else in your career. It's all about your networks.

Talk to your head of HR

Most likely, the human resources leader at your own company has a relationship with the major executive search firms, having hired such a firm to find the people who populate your executive boardroom. Once you've made the case with your CEO for joining a board (and gotten him to make some calls on your behalf), meet with your HR leaders as well. "Your HR leader can call his recruiter friends and say, 'We have a great CIO and we'd like him to get some board experience. These are his skills; this is where he could contribute. Can you keep him in mind?'"

HR leaders have some leverage with executive recruiters. Get them to put the word out to their executive search networks so that your name is bandied about in the right circles. "I received many calls when I was CIO of Campbell, precisely because of this," says Wright. "My head of HR gave out my name and people would call me for board work. It is an effective path, because your HR partner is in a position to describe you very well."

Wait until you retire

When I was in third grade, my classmates and I were given the assignment of calculating our age in the year 2000. When I discovered that I would be thirty-four, I was horrified. How, at thirty-four years of age, would I enjoy all the hovercrafts and Mars adventures that would surely be in daily operation? I would be so *old*. I think that, similarly, many of us assume that when we retire, all we will want to do is travel and grow tomatoes. But that may not be the case. You may actually want to continue to engage as an executive, and board service could be just the thing. "Boards of directors may be concerned that a sitting CIO does not have the capacity to contribute to a board," says Wright. "The CIO's own CEO might have the same concerns. You may have a better shot at a board appointment if you wait until you retire."

Join the board of a not-for-profit organization

Doreen Wright sat on the boards for a large number of not-for-profits before she sat on her first public company board. "You get a lot out of the experience," she says. "These boards are not as professional or business oriented, and of course you don't get paid, but you do get some pretty great experience." Nonprofit boards are still boards, and they exhibit many of the same dynamics as their corporate counterparts. "How do you work together? How do you delegate responsibilities? How do you get things done? Nonprofits offer a chance to learn how to work as a governing body," says Wright.

In addition to allowing you to contribute to something you care about and give back to your community, nonprofits offer a path to new networks as well. "Who do you think sits on nonprofit boards?" asks Wright. "All of the business leaders who share your passion. A bunch of CEOs and CFOs will be sitting on the board of your city's ballet company; these are the people who hire public company board members."

Do you go to your college alumni events? Do you still network with the members of your MBA class? In addition to nonprofits, there are other natural networks that you can leverage to widen your circle of friends. Bob DeRodes has participated in a number of local nonprofit boards, and values the experience. "You need to join a local board to get a sense of what a board does, how it operates, takes minutes, calls to order, all of that," he says. "And technology people are in high demand at not-for-profits. These organizations are small and need IT advice."

Do the Google test

About a year ago, I Googled myself (a phrase that still sounds slightly off-color to me, no matter how often I hear it), and I found something quite scandalous. Right at the top of the search results page was a story about a twenty-two-year-old woman from Iowa named Martha Heller who had engaged in a fairly bizarre entrepreneurial pursuit. (That's all common decency will allow me to publish here. Go use your research skills to figure out the rest of the story yourself.) So here I am, publishing consistently for more than twelve years, and I am upstaged but one wacky woman doing one wacky thing. So, I hired a search engine optimization consultant who fixed that particular situation.

If you do the Google test yourself, what do you find? The first thing that someone recruiting for a board are going to do is research the referrals they are given. Whatever you find when you Google yourself is what they will find. Recruiters and board members will want to know if you gave the commencement address at a local university or if you've established a new leadership development program in your company. "Get out there, speak, get published, get noticed," advises Wright. "You have to work to get yourself known."

Make sure you really want this

You know the joke: What's the difference between an introverted CIO and an extroverted CIO? The introverted CIO looks at his shoes when he talks to you. The extroverted CIO looks at *your* shoes. "Some of the most brilliant and successful people in technology are just not great conversationalists," says DeRodes. If your clear preference is to read a book rather than walk into a room filled with people, you might not belong on a board.

Conclusion

The fact is getting a paid directorship on a corporate board is really hard. No matter the strength of your desire, if you don't have the right background, track record, credentials, and networks, it may simply not happen for you. Join a nonprofit and enjoy the new experience, the new people, and the opportunity to give back.

However, if you do have a background that traverses IT and P&L leadership, if you are CIO of a respected company whose CEO values board experience in his executives, and if you have great networking skills, then start your board appointment plan now. Enlist the executive leadership team of your company and set a strategic plan to secure your first corporate board appointment. Compliance, risk, innovation, and mobility are all taking center stage for almost every industry on the planet. There has never been a better time for CIOs to serve on boards, and it is high time that boards saw the light.

11

The CIO Career Path Paradox

Sometimes, especially as my daughters move into their teens, I think back on my days in college. As I rummage through memories of keggers and coffee, courses and Kahlua, I worry that I could have done more. Did I make the most of every learning opportunity? Did I push myself as hard as I could have? Did I capitalize on my parents' investment in those expensive four years? Or did I privilege partying over pedagogy one too many times? Would I be a better person if I had embraced every learning opportunity that college had to offer?

If we try hard, we can create an analogy here to the CIO role. CIOs are uniquely positioned to move into different chairs around the executive table, but only if they seize on the opportunities that present themselves now. Just as I did in college, CIOs can do what it takes to get a solid B+ and still sleep in. Or they can, as my father used to say, "Leave no stone unturned," and enjoy the opportunities they create with all their hard work.

From CIO to COO

Let's start with the COO position. But before we do, I will offer a disclaimer. In this chapter, I do not mean to imply, in any way, that there is something wrong with a career spent as a CIO. I meet CIOs every day who are thrilled with their jobs. While these CIOs would consider changing companies from time to time, they are completely fulfilled by their CIO position and are not gunning for a change.

At the same time, a considerable group among my CIO friends would like to replace that "I" with a new letter. They respect and admire the "E" but they recognize the considerable challenges in obtaining it. They typically want nothing to do with the "F," and they do not consider the "S" to be a step forward. But that "O," that beautiful "O." With its promise of more power, better compensation, increased status, and an unquestioned place at the table, "O" is a letter they deem worth fighting for.

CIOs who move into the COO role are still in the minority, a fact that owes much to the CIO Paradox. How can executives who touch every part of the business, from order to delivery to HR to finance, who are responsible for standards, QA, cost reduction, and process improvement, and who know their company's operations intimately, *not* be considered for a COO position? We have already discussed a number of answers to the question throughout this book. But, whatever the reason, CIOs who have made their careers on the basis of their technology excellence will need to distance themselves from it at a certain point in their career.

Raise your hand for enterprise initiatives

Typically, the CIO to COO journey happens as follows: the CIO takes the job with some understanding that she will have the opportunity to reach beyond IT and assume an enterprise leadership role in an area like call center operations or customer care or strategic planning. She does just that and tells her boss she is ready and able to move into the COO position at the appropriate time. That time comes along, and she is anointed.

If you did not come onboard to your current position with a clear understanding of your COO career path, you still have options, of course. The first is to look for a new CIO role where you can onboard differently. The second is to skip that part and look for a COO position at another company. This move is not impossible, but it's tough. CEOs are often unwilling to take a chance on someone who has not already performed the role in its entirety.

The third option, and probably the best, is to look around your current company and see where you can expand your reach. Obviously, if you aren't successfully delivering IT to your company now, you should stop reading this chapter and get to it. But if you are a respected and valued member of the executive team, you may be ready to start building your COO résumé.

Back in 1993, Bill Wray joined Citizens Financial Group where he ran credit and risk management. Several years into the role, he was asked to move into technology to create a project management function over the bank's Y2K program. "The Y2K program got me the CIO job," he says. After he became CIO in 2000, he continued to add a series of operational functions, including check processing, customer service, and procurement to his plate. "Citizens didn't have a COO position," Wray says. "I was as close to the COO role as anyone."

In 2009, Wray joined Blue Cross & Blue Shield of Rhode Island (BCBSRI) as CIO. As at Citizens, he started with responsibility for IT but then picked up core operational areas like customer service, claims processing, and continuous improvement. Last year, BCBSRI hired a new CEO who did a review of the executive team and asked Wray to take the COO position. When he stepped into the new role, Wray promoted one of his leaders into the CIO position and took on new responsibilities, including the clinical side of operations, client services, and the organization's for-profit wellness services subsidiary.

Wray didn't set out to become COO. "My career plans are about happiness," he says. "If I like what I'm doing and I'm getting fairly compensated, I am happy. I didn't come to work every day saying, 'I must be a COO.'" At the same time, Wray has always sought out responsibilities that extend beyond the traditional boundaries of IT. "I believe that people are defined by the problems they are asked to solve," says Wray. "I have always chafed at focusing solely on solving technical problems, when most of the important and interesting challenges are about something other than technology."

Greg Carmichael offers another example of a CIO reaching beyond IT. After serving for several years in a number of IT leadership roles at GE, Carmichael became CIO for Emerson Electric. In 2003, he joined Fifth Third Bancorp as CIO. "My job was to get the IT organization to a place where we could acquire and integrate other banks and open new branches," he says. "We accomplished that in a short amount of time, so I started to take on new responsibilities." Carmichael took on areas beyond IT, including investment operations, Six Sigma, global sourcing, and program management. In 2006, his title changed to COO to reflect those responsibilities and to anticipate his role in future initiatives.

His boss, president of Fifth Third Bancorp, had recognized Carmichael's leadership qualities, and when it was time to choose a COO, he turned to Carmichael.

Carmichael agrees that reaching beyond IT is a critical step in securing a COO role. "Step in as acting CFO when there is turnover in finance, or lead the recruitment effort for a new head of HR. Demonstrate enterprise leadership in your day job and you're on the road to your next position," says Carmichael.

When Carmichael joined Fifth Third, he saw the company had not matured in its sourcing strategy, an area he knew well from his years in manufacturing. "My recommendation was that we build a sourcing organization," says Carmichael, "and I offered to do it myself."[5]

Go for continuous improvement

When Wray was at Citizens, he and his team were managing a number of integrations, with the mandate to make significant cuts to the budget. "This was way beyond the typical 5 percent, and I didn't know how to do it," he says. "So this guy I know said, 'There's this Lean Six Sigma thing,' and that got me started on continuous improvement." When Wray joined BCBSRI as CIO, he saw that there was no real continuous improvement discipline in the company—no structured approach to improving cost, customer service, and risk management based on Six Sigma principles. "I said, 'We need this, and I'm going to sponsor it.'"

As his company's continuous improvement champion, Wray was able to use his CIO skills to provide enterprise leadership at a different level. "If, like most CIOs, you are good at project management and good at driving structured change, you will be good at being your company's continuous improvement champion," says Wray. And because these skills are the same as those you use in IT project delivery, you don't have to get permission to practice. "Continuous improvement is a natural extension of your CIO role. It makes you a better leader, and it will give you more than technology problems to solve," Wray says.

Don't be shy

We have all been told, from the time we were children, that actions speak louder than words and that if we work hard enough, the fruits of all of that labor will be bestowed to us. While that may often be true, if you are after the COO ring, you need to speak up. I have interviewed a number of CIOs who have become COO, and every one of them communicated their intentions to their CEOs. Wray concurs, "It is always a good idea to tell people what you want," he says. "Let it be known that you are interested in taking on the larger, more interesting problems. Sometimes you have to do things on a pro bono basis, but if you are generous with your skills, the rewards will come back to you."

Get ready to "be" the business

Wray says that his time as CIO prepared him for much of what he now encounters as COO, but there are some significant differences. "As CIO, you could be successful as an executive who could manage IT and *be sensitive* to the business," he says. "But as COO, you have to *be* the business. It is tempting to continue to solve technology problems, but if you do, you will never be embraced as the COO and your new CIO will never grow into the role." As CIO, your business partners are your customers, and it is your job to support and enable business change. "But as COO, you have to engender change at a very different level," says Wray. "Now, the meat of your job is to come up with the business strategies that other people enable and support. You have to get that part of your brain working. It's no longer, 'How can I help you?' It's a different kind of conversation."

Be prepared to diversify your management style

As CIO, you managed IT people, and dealt with the rich array of personalities that can exist in an IT organization. But as COO, your teams include a much more diverse group, which may well require you to change your management style. "When I was CIO of Citizens, I ran an organization of four thousand people, but they were a technology and operations team," says Wray. "Today, I am managing nurses, who work with individuals on individual problems. I am used to coaching people to work at the portfolio level, not the transactional level. I have to figure out how to do that."

From CIO to CEO

The path from CIO to CEO is certainly less travelled than the road to COO, but it does exist, and CIOs who use their position to build their CEO résumés are the most likely candidates. "When you are CIO, you are practicing some of the skills necessary to be a CEO," says Mike Kistner, who was CIO of Best Western International and then COO and CEO of Pegasus Solutions, a provider of reservation and distribution technology and financial and marketing services to the hospitality industry. "As CIO, you need to be great at strategic planning, finance, HR, sales, and marketing," he says. "And with businesses using more data and becoming much more scientific in the way they run, someone with a technology background could be a great candidate for the CEO role."

The problem, of course, is that the board of directors still may not see it that way. "What's ironic is that, precisely because a CIO has been successful in his or her role, the board sometimes has a bias that once you have the technology view, you can never transcend it," says Kistner. The CIO Paradox that Kistner refers to, of course, is that once you're in IT you can't get out. By obtaining the considerable skills and focus necessary to run an IT organization, you brand yourself as a technology person and that brand becomes your albatross. But, as Kistner and others have proven, this is a paradox that can be broken.

Michael Capellas, former CIO and CEO of Compaq, CEO of MCI and CEO of First Data, and currently Chairman of VCE, was one of the first and certainly most famous CIOs to break the CIO Career Path Paradox. He sees plenty of reasons for CIOs to make the leap: "CIOs have to be experts at solving complex problems. They have to be precise and experienced planners, they have to spring into operational mode, and they have to be more global than their peers."[6]

So what can CIOs do now to prepare themselves for the corner office?

Learn to balance internal and external demands

"The CEO has a much larger group of external constituencies than the CIO, including the board, investors, partners, and customers, and has to know when to prioritize the internal versus the external," says Capellas. "When I became CEO of Compaq, my first priority was to be the voice of the customer and to go on a hundred customer visits and see everyone. I thought that it was absolutely the right thing to do until I realized I was on the verge of being an absentee leader."

Change up your management style

Capellas reiterates Bill Wray's caution that, when you take on teams outside of IT, you should think hard about your management style and make some adjustments. This is even more important when you are CEO. "As CEO, you have a far more diverse group of people to manage—HR, finance, product development, sales—and you have to learn to relate to them in different ways," says Capellas.

Run IT like a business

For CIOs who truly aspire to the CEO seat, Capellas offers an exercise. "Think of yourself as the CEO of your own business where demand for your services will always be higher than your ability to supply them," he says, "and everybody is an expert in your consumer business but nobody understands your enterprise business." According to Capellas, if you can manage those significant business conflicts in a way that keeps all your customers happy, you will have developed the relationship and sales skills to make it as CEO.

Develop your "minors"

As a CIO with a "major" in technology, you may have quite a few "minors" to develop before you are ready for general management. During the late '90s, Michael Curran was promoted from CIO of Scudder Stevens & Clark (Zurich Scudder Investments) to a series of general management roles, including COO. In 2001, he became CIO of the Boston Stock Exchange, and in 2005, he became its CEO.

"All CEOs have a major in something, and they've had to build their knowledge of other functions off of that core," says Curran. CIOs should do the same, he says. "Take a course in contract law and negotiation, learn balance sheets, learn something about marketing. If you're working globally, read a book about each country you're visiting, learn a foreign language." With a serious day job on your hands, you cannot expect to develop expertise in each of your company's domains, but you can, according to Curran, "get good enough so that you don't embarrass yourself."[7]

Scale your conception of systems relationships

"CIOs live in a systems world, and they understand the interdependencies among the elements of the systems—the hardware, the apps, the networks, the third-party vendors," says Curran. "If you can scale that notion of interdependencies to a broader level that includes boards and governance, product management, people, services, and sales, you will be able to adopt the CEO mind-set."

Plan a transitional move into general management

From 1996 to 2000, Chris Lofgren served as CIO of trucking company Schneider National. At the same time, he became president of its logistics business. In 2000, he was promoted to COO. He became president and CEO two years later. "With the exception of a technology company, it is highly unlikely that a company will promote a CIO directly to the CEO position," he says. "It makes more sense that a CIO would aim for a role running a business unit—one that is driven more by information—before attempting the CEO role."[8]

Embrace variety

Marc West is CEO of Mamasource, a social networking service for mothers. That's a far cry from his start as a programmer in the military. West left the service and joined a regional bank in network engineering. He helped the bank roll out ATMs, a new technology at the time. When the bank closed, West led the effort to wind down IT. "We all talk about the importance of managing growth," says West. "But you learn a lot about intellectual property and other assets when you have to shut something down."

When he left the bank, West joined the corporate group at Mobil Oil, where he worked on early use of client/server architecture. "Our challenge was to learn how to turn data into information to support a rapidly changing business model," says West.

After Mobil, West ran a financial services consulting practice for Oracle in New York City, where he picked up P&L management as a skill and then joined Quick & Reilly, a discount brokerage house, as VP of technology. "What I learned is that on Wall Street, information is power and information depends on good technology," says West. "You either made a lot of money for your customer or lost it, in large part on the basis of your technology."

Fleet Bank bought Quick & Reilly, and West joined Move.com, a dot-com start-up in the real estate industry, as CTO and head of business operations. "We built the business from nothing to $70 million and sold it to Homestore. We merged our platform with theirs. That was an amazing learning opportunity but also a lot of hard work," says West.[9]

By the year 2000, West had worked in the fields of military, financial services, energy, and high-tech. He built technology, ran a P&L, grew organizations, and shrunk them. He had worked in small companies where he wore many hats and in huge companies where he had a very defined role.

My perspective as a recruiter is that, while consistency, focus, depth, and loyalty are important, it is also true that the greater diversity of roles you have had in your career, the more career options you will have open to you. This is not to say that you want a jumpy résumé, where you have not lasted anywhere for more than two years, but if you can balance tenure with variety, you will have a much better shot at new executive roles, including CEO.

Know what you are good at

In 2000, West took his first bone fide CIO position when he joined Electronic Arts, a leading provider of video games. "They were a $1 billion company that wanted to be 3X in three years," he says. "That was their battle cry, but their technology was a significant limiter." West shored up both IT operations and the development group which helped grow the company to $3.2 billion. "I played a lot of video games," he says. In the end, West decided to move on, because video games were not a passion for him, so he would have a hard time moving into a general management position. "I'm not truly a gamer," he says, "So I was not the best person to run a production studio." From his experience at Electronic Arts, West gained a powerful personal insight: "There is a difference between universal capabilities—like leadership and communication—and business specialist skills," he says. "At Electronic Arts, if you are not a gamer, you cannot convince yourself that you can become one and grow into a general management role. You need to know what you're good at and be good at it. It's a learned instinct thing."

Use the two-way mirror approach

After four years at Electronic Arts, West joined H&R Block as CIO. Again, he found a company whose technology was a barrier to growth. "They had some interesting problems," he says. "How do you hire a hundred thousand seasonal employees? How do you reacquire twenty-one million customers every year? If you miss nine days of revenue at the beginning of the tax season, the business is unprofitable for the entire year."

After improving the business platform at H&R Block, West moved from CIO to the corporate operations role, with the title of group president for corporate. In that position, he created a new product offering and business platform by partnering with retail store operations to develop a new business unit, H&R Block Commercial Markets, which would provide tax preparation software to mom-and-pop tax advisers, and which brought in an additional 380,000 new customers.

West came up with the idea for Commercial Markets during an RFP process for some tax preparation software he was evaluating to support the business. "We used that RFP to review the major software providers to our competitors," says West. "From that software review, we learned a lot about the independent market and what our next move could be."

West calls this approach a "two-way mirror" model: in the course of evaluating technology for your own business, you ask the right questions to gain insights about how your competitors are using that technology. "Every time you look at a technology, consider not just what it does for you, but what it does for your competitors," says West. "Then you are thinking like a CEO."

Running a Technology Company

One of the most travelled routes from CIO to CEO is via the technology company. As longtime customers of technology providers, CIOs know the products and development process, they know the business—from the customer view—and they've sat through enough presentations to know how (or how not) to sell technology solutions. And if they've been networking with their peers, they should have a good customer target list as well.

"In 1985, I had an epiphany," says Mike Kistner, former CEO of Pegasus Solutions. "I was a senior developer at Super 8 Motels, working on a general ledger program, and I realized that the date fields had two digits. I thought, 'This will be a nightmare in 2000 and will take some real development work to solve.' Around this time, one of the vice presidents saw me cranking away and said to me, 'Is this what you want to do your whole life, write code?' Right then and there, I vowed to get out of IT and to do it before Y2K."

That same vice president asked Kistner to get up from his keyboard and take a look at the company's call center, which was running on a manual system. He asked Kistner to evaluate the situation, which he did, and he came up with a new model for how to forecast call center capacity. "That made me realize that I had some financial and analytical skills," says Kistner, who was promoted to call center manager. From there, as Super 8 began to sell new technology to its franchises, Kistner was tapped to present the offerings to large groups. "I was the kid who hated speech class," says Kistner, "and I find myself at a convention in Phoenix addressing fifteen hundred people. I got through it, and to this day I do not look forward to public speaking, but the experience showed people that I had the ability to articulate a complex technical solution to the average hotel owner."

When Super 8 hired a new CEO, he made Kistner his COO, responsible for IT, reservations, franchise services, HR, convention planning, and a number of other areas. "I'm sitting in his office and looking at this sheet of paper that lists all of these things that I'm now responsible for," says Kistner. "It was one of those bizarre situations."

Get out of IT

A few years later, Super 8 was acquired by HFS and then by Cendant; Kistner continued to lead IT as well as reservations and other operational areas. In 2000, Kistner joined Best Western as CIO and, following in a tradition of holding blended roles, picked up distribution as well. Five years later, he joined Pegasus Solutions as a full-fledged COO and then became CEO in 2008.

Go for an operations position first

"A great stepping-stone from CIO to CEO is the EVP of operations," says Kistner. "It's a gradual transition. You can expand both your horizons and the perception people have of your leadership skills while you hold onto IT." But once you have secured that operations title, your work isn't done. "I will tell you that, regardless of how many years you've been a COO, if you came up through the technology path, people will still talk to you as if you have a technology bent to everything you approach. Even when you've solved huge business problems and had many public speaking engagements, the board of directors will still view you as a technologist."

As CEO of a technology provider, the board's perception of you as a technologist may be as much of an asset as a liability, but according to Kistner, time can solve the problem for you. "There gets to be a point you've been a CEO long enough that people just come to see you as a traditional CEO with a broad background," says Kistner. "The economy plunged within a month of my becoming CEO, so I had to focus pretty intensely on the finances of the business. People just started to look at me now as someone to lead them through difficult times."

Polish your leadership skills

"As CIOs, I think we sometimes mistake project management skills for real leadership skills," says Kistner. When you are focused on project delivery, it is critical that everyone follow a road map with strict attention to roles, budgets, and time lines. "If you are providing real leadership, you want teams that are not necessarily following your direction.

You need a team that will challenge you, but who will provide the innovation you would never get from a team that just falls in line."

Make sure you love to sell

When I am coaching CIOs who want to move into CEO roles, I usually ask them about their sales experience. They often tell me that, while they have not actually sold products or services to external customers, they have a track record of selling business cases, requests for funding, and "vision." That track record is impressive, to be sure, but it is different from sales. "CEOs sell," says Kistner. "And that can be a real transition from being a CIO. If, at heart, you are a technologist, you will want to tout the capabilities of your product instead of selling your solution. If you are at all uncomfortable with selling, you will have a tough time as CEO."

Fill in your skills gaps

Sean O'Neill is Chairman of Newmarket International, a sales and catering solutions provider for the hospitality industry. He was the CIO of ITT Sheraton when he realized that he wanted to broaden his aspirations. "I was creating a ceiling for myself as CIO. I wanted to have broader influence over decision making and decided to pursue a different path."

During interviews with his next employer, travel vendor Grand Circle, O'Neill talked about "how we had transformed information technology at ITT Sheraton into a business function that was integrated with the business. They knew that, while I was coming to them as a CIO, my motivation was to be on the business side."

Grand Circle hired O'Neill as CIO, with the understanding that he would soon add EVP of operations to his role. Several years later, in 2001, he joined Newmarket as CEO. "I chose a technology provider strategically," says O'Neill. "I wanted to stay close to what I knew best. I had the experience of being a consumer of these products and could get up to speed very quickly."

O'Neill's advice: "Become a student of the skill sets required to run a business. As CIO, you have access to a wide variety of leaders both inside your company and out. Interact with those people and start to understand where the gaps are in your own skills."

He found, for example, that while he had a good grasp of functions like accounting, human resources, and sales, he needed a better understanding of the financials. "I would risk looking like someone who doesn't get it by raising my hand in a meeting and asking, 'Why did we use this debt structure?'" he says. "I would anticipate my next meeting with our CFO and prepare questions."[10]

Conclusion

The recurring advice that CIOs turned CEOs or COOs gave during our interviews was "Recognize your strengths and be careful what you wish for." This points us to a particularly enduring CIO Paradox: *That which makes for a great technologist, can be precisely what makes for a lousy CEO.* The DNA necessary for thinking through the details of a complex technical problem may be different from the DNA necessary to get a market excited about a new company or product. Same goes for accountability. To quote Marc West, "On time and on budget is not the same as satisfying customers and shareholders while generating meaningful revenue." If you are the exception to that rule, and you have mastered the skills of IT leadership and you have the *je ne sais quoi* of a GM, you have no reason not to move up and out of the CIO role—if that is what you want to do. The number of success stories of CIOs who have followed that path is only growing.

12

The Future of the CIO Role

In my first few years as a staff writer at *CIO* magazine, we published a number of articles on the future of the CIO role. My favorite was a cover story on the threat that the emerging CTO position posed to the CIO. *CIO* magazine has always had the best designers in the business, and for the cover, they designed this creepy-looking creature that peered through a dark, misty haze like a wolf ready to devour its prey.

Well, here I am at it again, prognosticating about what the next few years will hold for the IT executive. And I am not alone. A quick Google search for "the future of the CIO" or "the death of the CIO" brings up pages of articles on similar topics (with loads of comments begging that the debate be put out of its misery).

The writers of those comments do have a point: has any executive position gone under the microscope as often as the CIO? Do we read articles on the future of the CFO or COO or the head of HR? Maybe a few, but the CIO's role has been poked and prodded and manhandled since the early 1980s when the position first came into existence.

Perhaps we scrutinize the CIO position so often because of the rapid pace of technology change. The basic principles of sales, marketing, and finance are as old as the hills, whereas technology platforms and paradigms shift every eighteen months or so. How can we hope to understand the CIOs' role when the ground shifts so often under their feet? Perhaps we speculate about the CIO's future because, compared with every other executive function, the CIO's is the toughest to pin down and understand. (The senior leadership team finally understands software-as-a-service, but now we are talking about platform-as-a-service. What on earth is that?)

Well, far be it for me to buck the trend and write an entire book about CIOs without including a chapter on the role's future. So, let's get to it.

During my interviews for this book, I made the following statement to a number of CIOs: "In ten years, someone else will be CIO of your company," (and then I had to pause to let them sigh with relief as they imagined an existence free of the weight of IT infrastructure). Or, as one CIO said, "If I'm not retired in ten years, shoot me."

And then I asked, "How will the new CIO's job be different from yours?" Some thought that the CIO role would go away completely as the new generation of leaders became comfortable with outsourcing almost all of IT. Others thought that the CIO role would stick around and be relatively unchanged—new technologies, same responsibilities. But the majority described a future in which the CIO role exists but with a focus that is different enough from its current one that it might benefit from a new title. What follows is a veritable potpourri of technology leadership roles, from the perspective of those who are doing the job today.

Chief Innovation Officer

CIOs have been driving productivity for decades. They got on the map, way back when, by making the business more efficient by automating some basic manual processes. Then they began delivering communication systems, like e-mail, which made everyone more productive. With

ERP, CIOs moved into the arena of business process change. Along the way, they also made good use of outsourcing for increased productivity and cost savings.

For each major evolution in the IT arena, CIOs have had to pick up different skills: technology, project management, change leadership, business process knowledge, and outsourcing. So, what now? What's the next frontier for technology-driven productivity? For many CIOs, the next frontier is in business model innovation. Right now, insurance-company CIOs are developing pedometer apps for their customers, and retail CIOs are letting consumers design their own jeans while they wait in line at the supermarket.

CIOs who have the "chameleon factor" that I described in chapter 1 will be able to do more than change business processes; they will change the business. In a recent article in *CIO* magazine, Peter High, author of *World-Class IT: Why Businesses Succeed When IT Triumphs*, describes the evolution of CIOs into the innovator position as "CIO squared—the combination of chief information officer and chief innovation officer." His view is that, as companies are figuring out where to place innovation leadership in their companies, CIOs have the opportunity to take the mantle.

While innovation should be baked into the role of every executive, the CIO is well positioned to take the lead. "With the rise of social media, mobility, the consumerization of IT, big data, and business intelligence, IT-centered innovation is growing," says High. "IT leaders are well positioned to sit at the hub of discussions with the heads of business units and departments about the sources of innovation and the technology to support them."[11]

Chief Improvement Officer

With their program management and change leadership responsibilities, CIOs are ripe for the role of continuous improvement champion across the enterprise. As more IT functions are outsourced, and business leaders get comfortable with reaching to the cloud for their technology solutions, the CIO will be released from hands-on IT operations and free to make business processes across the company faster, better, and cheaper. In a number of companies, CIOs are working hard to add continuous improvement to their plates. If you don't have a continuous improvement champion in your company, you may want to raise your hand for the job. "I believe that future CIOs will have a real opportunity to broaden their influence beyond IT and take responsibility for things like quality and continuous improvement," says Ron Kifer, former CIO of Applied Materials. "What I would really like to see in ten years is CIOs becoming the modelers of change behavior, both inside of IT and out."

Jody Davids, CIO of Best Buy, agrees that CIOs' reach will extend beyond IT and will drive change across the enterprise. Thus, CIOs' relationships to their executive peers will change as well. "The next CIO will be focused less on pure technology and using technology to drive change to achieve organizational design and business process outcomes," she says. "Just as the lines between the CFO, COO, and CEO get blurred when they are at the executive table, the lines between IT and the CIO's other functional counterparts will blur as well. When we leave our offices and sit at the executive table, we will be indistinguishable from many of the other functional executives."[12]

Chief Intelligence Officer

In this version of the CIO role, the "I" stands for the ability to take data and turn it into actionable business intelligence, whether technology is involved or not. Wayne Shurts, CIO of the $38 billion grocery company SUPERVALU, recently developed a solution for improving sales and ensuring the freshness of fruits and vegetables in his stores' produce departments. He supplied sales data to store managers so that they could allocate shelf space accordingly. I asked him what technology he had used: RFID? Smartphones? "Sticky tape," he said.

Many CIOs have evolved beyond the "I have a technology hammer, so everything is a technology nail" mind-set and now see their role as serving up information to solve business problems. Sometimes the right business-intelligence solution has no technology component at all.

"Part of the CIO's role today is around stewardship of information," says John Dick, CIO of Towers Watson. "That will become even more of a focus in the future. The underlying technologies are going to change, but our role to distill the data and help our business make decisions faster and better than our competition will always be important."

Chief Shared Services Officer

In companies where business units are prone to making their own technology investments or where technology, despite advances in cloud and mobility, will continue to be a keep-the-lights-on activity, the CIO role will be to manage a smorgasbord of software and managed services providers to ensure security, support, integration, and efficiency. "As organizations become more dependent upon third parties, the role will become more of a contract management function," says Lynden Tennison, CIO of Union Pacific. "This role will be most pronounced in companies where the CEO does not consider technology to be highly strategic."

Erez Yarkoni, CIO of T-Mobile, agrees that Chief Shared Services Officer is the destiny for some CIOs. "CIOs who spend most of their time as operators, running infrastructure and data centers and large teams, are going to be asked to do things cheaper and faster every year," he says. "But what traditionally happens with operations, like manufacturing, is that it gets moved to a place where it benefits from scale or lower labor costs, as opposed to being managed within the organization. Eventually, infrastructure and software will go that way. In this scenario, which has already begun in many companies, you really don't need a CIO. The function can be managed out of business operations."

Doreen Wright, formerly CIO of Campbell Soup, shares this vision.

"For large companies, there will be almost no IT in-house at all: no data center, network services groups, application development or maintenance," she says. "When it comes to running IT, companies will have a few business analysts in-house and will spend most of their time doing big negotiations with their outsourcers." If they play their cards right, CIOs who excel at running IT as a support function, will expand their roles into other shared functions, like legal, procurement and HR.

Chief Technology Officer

I have been talking to CIOs about their roles, accomplishments, and hopes and dreams for thirteen years now (and yet I remain so young!). And I have always been struck by the fact that our conversations are so rarely about technology. We talk about change management, people development, project management, executive relationships, outsourcing—but very rarely about hardware or software. But lately, our conversations have been changing. Lately, I am finding that CIOs are flexing their technologist muscles again.

One of my favorite questions to ask CIOs during an introductory conversation is, "If you were at a roundtable of your peers, and you could pick the topic of discussion what would it be? What are you grappling with in your organization so much so that you would like to hear how your CIO peers are handling the same challenge? " What I have noticed in the past twelve months is that these CIOs' responses are less and less often about people or business strategy. They are about technology! One CIO responded, "I would love to talk to other CIOs about their architecture and how they are integrating consumer devices with their back-end systems." And, "We have ten thousand employees, with 60 percent of them in sales. How do we deliver data over mobile devices to them in a secure way?" I just spoke with a CIO yesterday who had been spending her time educating her team on form factors. To be sure, these CIOs are focused on strategy and growth and external customers, too, but with all of the technology innovation that is taking place even at this moment, CIOs are more focused on the actual technology than they have been in the past few years.

As Lynden Tennison puts it, "One version of the future CIO is the technical CIO. This is the CIO who is expected to be more wired into the technical community, to know how tools and standards are evolving. This CIO will bring leading-edge technical competence to the table, which will help differentiate the business."

Chief Orchestration Officer

Tom Conophy, former CIO of InterContinental Hotels Group, sees the future CIO as leading functions very similar to the strategy teams that are in companies now. "It will be a small cadre of what I call 'big fore-headed people,'" he says. "They are forward-looking thought leaders in their domain and are sitting on top of maybe ten or eleven major contracts with cloud providers. Their role is as a conductor in the construction and integrity of solutions."

Barbra Cooper, former CIO of Toyota Motor North America, agrees with the "CIO as conductor" metaphor. "The CIO will evolve into the role of chief architect, who can see the future of how technology is changing the business and can be the master integrator of all of the moving parts."

Chief Engineering Officer

Today, every company is a technology company, whether its business is health care, retail, telecom, or financial services. In fact, we are in the midst of a technology renaissance, with companies engaged in a products frenzy. "All different kinds of companies will need to reinvent their strategies with software-based products," says T-Mobile CIO Erez Yarkoni. "They will need a new kind of engineering executive to lead that effort."

In Yarkoni's view, CIOs of companies that are beefing up their technology product lines will have three options. The first is to manage back office systems as described in the chief Shared Services Officer section above. The second is to embrace their software development backgrounds (if they have them) and architect the technology platform that runs, like a shared service, through all of the company's products. In this "Chief Engineering Officer" role, the technology background that has always been a bit of a liability for a CIO (compared with a business background) is suddenly an asset. And the third option is to run a technology products business, as described in the next section.

Chief Product Officer

In Yarkoni's view, the future is bright for CIOs who have a background in business. With most companies shifting to a focus on technology products and services, CIOs who have served in the business and in IT, will enjoy a wealth of opportunity. "CIOs who have experience with sales, marketing, and brand creation can ride the technology products wave into product or P&L management," says Yarkoni. These executives, who came to the CIO role with all the skills necessary to run a business, will have picked up software development, operations management, and a deep knowledge of IT. That's a mighty powerful skill set to bring to a new technology products business.

Conclusion

When technology innovation produces the need for new executive skills, it can take a while for companies to figure out where to put those executives and the functions they manage. E-business was a classic example of this where companies were not certain whether the function belonged in marketing, technology, or in the individual lines of business. Today, it is this "products" focus that is emerging in companies all over the industry spectrum. I see "products" as a major catalyst or impediment to the CIO role. So many industries, like retail, hospitality, financial services, healthcare, and media are shifting their traditional business model to one much more focused on delivering services via innovative technology channels. In some companies, the CIO remains a critical part of the strategy team and a leader in making technology investment decisions. In many of these, product development reports right up to the CIO. In others, accountability for the development of technology products shifts to the business, and the CIO winds up providing shared services like data centers, e-mail, and ERP to these new product leaders. Which role the CIO takes depends on many factors, including her credibility with her executive peers.

But regardless of how the "products issue" shakes out in your company, if you can deliver great IT, you will find solid ground in this new era of computing. One thing is certain: There will be plenty of need for executives who understand technology and how it makes a business better.

Breaking the Paradox

During my interviews for this book, and in my conversations with other CIOs over the years, I have found that there are certain approaches, practices, and philosophies that are common to successful CIOs. These CIOs have not done away with the many contradictions of IT leadership. As I mentioned in the opening of this book, the CIO Paradox is here to stay. But these CIOs have managed to be successful regardless.

The phrase I like to use to describe the phenomenon of success in the face of lousy odds is "breaking the paradox," and this concluding chapter is dedicated to that concept. I have compiled these common "traits of successful CIOs" into a checklist for you to review, and perhaps, to share with the aspiring CIOs in your organization. My hope is that you, and they, can glean direction, inspiration, and a few good ideas from this list. Some of the items, like leadership and communication, appear on every "CIO Critical Competencies" roundup, while others, I hope, are new. Either way, these ideas come from CIOs who have spent years thinking over their challenges. If you can check the box next to every item, chances are you have broken the CIO Paradox and are destined for greatness.

Your Breaking the Paradox Checklist

☐ *Develop blended executives.*   Without good people, you will never be able to deliver on the maximum potential of IT, and your own career will suffer as a result. As Barbra Cooper, Kevin Hart, and Lynden Tennison have all demonstrated, good staff development programs have been a critical element of their own success as IT leaders. IT people are a unique breed, and they need to develop a demanding blend of business, technology, and interpersonal skills. This is more the case now than ever before. Most companies are currently in need of IT people with two heads: one for business and one for technology. Last time I checked, cloning is still an imperfect science, so you will need to grow your own. A program that rotates your people into business roles will go a long way toward giving you a set of executives with a blended skills portfolio. Mike Capone bases much of his success as CIO of ADP on his own rotational experience as a business unit leader. "I lived on the other side of the equation and saw firsthand how IT impacted my business," he says. "I don't know how I could be a CIO without having rotated through the business."

There is a war for talent heading our way, and while executive recruiters will always be happy to take your calls, you don't want to have to go outside too often for your top people. Cooper, Hart, and Tennison did not wait for someone else to build a development program for them. They saw the need and made it happen. To quote Barbra Cooper: "I actually drafted a written eighteen-month contract between two officers of the company, one on the business side, and me, the CIO, which outlined the terms and conditions of the rotational assignment."

What is one clear way to determine whether your staff development program is a success? It is when you can claim some role in mentoring people who have gone on to become CIOs.

☐ *Be good at recruiting.* Even with great leadership development programs in place, you will find yourself in the market for new IT people from time to time. The most successful CIOs are those who have turned their business process reengineering lens onto their approach to recruiting.

"Rock star" candidates are phenomenally talented people: they are the world's future CIOs and they are happy in their jobs. It takes a lot for us recruiters to get them to consider your open position. Don't squander your chance of securing these assets through poor recruiting project management. There is a direct correlation between our success as recruiters and our clients' responsiveness, clarity, and willingness to put recruiting high on their list of priorities. Good people are a limited resource; your recruiting process should be a competitive advantage.

☐ *Get rid of the context.* If you grew up in IT operations, IT operations is what you know best. It served as the foundation of your success, and it is where you know you excel. But if you cling to the past and spend your time doing what vendors can do for you, you will fail. A theme in almost every interview I conducted for this book (and seen most clearly in comments made by Ron Kifer and Tom Murphy), is that the faster you can differentiate the core— your company's and IT team's critical differentiators—from the context—those commodity activities that you can pay someone to take off of your plate—the more successful you will be.

And with this new era of computing upon us, the core versus context equation may be changing. CIOs who have broken the paradoxes of strategy versus operations and cost versus innovation, and even archivist versus futurist, have figured out the lesson that Tom Murphy followed at AmerisoureBergen: "Our job is to get as much iron and heavy assets out of our facilities as possible that we can quickly move to the new platform paradigm."

Kevin Horner, former CIO of Alcoa concurs with Kifer on this strategy. "If you are a CIO and you own and operate most of your own infrastructure, you are a technology manager, not a CIO," he says. "It's like changing the oil in your car; maybe you can do it yourself, but why would you?" Horner accepts that for some companies, their infrastructure is their competitive differentiator, but for the vast majority, this is not the case. "If the processes you support are taking orders and paying people and doing accounts payable, you do not want to be spending any mental or operational energy on those activities," he says. "Your job is to separate out the activities that create advantage for your company, focus on them, and push the things into the market that the market has proven it can do as well as you."

☐ *Reach beyond IT.*   CIOs are picking up new titles left and right. We see "CIO and VP of customer care," and "CIO and VP of strategic planning" all the time. Whether they take on an additional title or not, it is time that CIOs apply their leadership far beyond the IT organization.

CIOs develop expertise in tough areas like project management, continuous improvement, people development, M&A, and strategic planning. These are disciplines from which almost every other department would benefit. CIOs who have broken the "IT and the Business" Paradox as discussed in chapter 5 simply assume that their leadership—and expertise—extends across the enterprise.

Brent Stacey knew he had broken the paradox when he was appointed to lead the company's management committee, and in turn, needed to appoint a deputy CIO to represent IT. Ron Kifer knew he had broken the paradox when his program and vendor management models were adopted across the enterprise. Barbra Cooper knew she had broken the paradox when her own executive rotational program was implemented company-wide. And as CIO, Bill Wray became his company's continuous improvement champion. In all of these scenarios, these CIOs stepped out of their IT box because they knew it was the right thing to do for the company. They didn't wait to be asked.

☐ *Move closer to the revenue.* When technology data is directly related to a company's products or services, the CIOs of those companies have a shot at driving revenue. CIOs of companies that build airplanes and power plants sometimes assume that the only way they will grow a company's revenues is through good business processes and technology support. That is not the attitude of Kim Hammonds, CIO of Boeing, or Ray Barnard, CIO of Fluor Corporation. To quote Hammonds, "I was recently at a session with twenty-five CIOs from the airlines, and I talked about mobile security and some of the work we are doing in that area. That has generated a lot of interest from these customers because they are looking for help in securing their mobile devices."

During Ray Barnard's first few months at Fluor, he used his own preexisting relationships to bring some sizeable new accounts to the company. In one way or another, every company is becoming a technology company. It is the perfect time for CIOs to get closer to the money.

☐ *Be a Chameleon.* The "DNA" of people who were attracted to technology twenty years ago may not lend itself to the work of today's CIOs: meeting with external customers, setting a vision, running an innovation group, and developing new ways to do business. CIOs who can make the leap from one set of responsibilities to the other have "the chameleon factor" and can move from a project management mind-set to an innovation mind-set. CIOs have been picking up new skills with every major evolutionary phase of IT. If you dig deep, you may just be able to do it again. But if you cannot, if your expertise is operational excellence, not business model innovation, be sure you hire the right senior people with skills to supplement your own, or find a company that needs what you have to offer.

☐ *Visit external customers.* According to *CIO* magazine's 2011 *State of the CIO* survey, only 9 percent of six hundred CIOs were spending any time studying market trends and customer needs, let alone getting out to visit customers. In the eleventh hour, I am bringing up yet another CIO Paradox: *You have accountability for all internal systems, yet you must spend more time with external customers.*

CIOs who have broken the paradox know as much about their 'Big C' customer as any other senior executive. When Mike Capone became CIO of ADP, he thought, "We are a great transaction processing company, but our customer demographic is changing to include younger people with mobile phones, so we need to work on our user experience." A major part of Capone's strategy in selling the executive committee on investing in user experience has been to rely on the voice of the customer. "At least 20 percent of my time is spent with our customers," he says. "I base my messages in the context of our clients. If I didn't, I'd be shouting into an empty valley."

The need to get out and spend time with customers can pose a real challenge to CIOs who have spent all of their time internally. "It takes a certain amount of social skills to get out in front of clients," says Capone. "When I started in this job, I was not an extrovert, and my clients were Intel, Microsoft, and Apple, who were not shy about their feedback. I had to work hard to develop the confidence and skills, like active listening, to get comfortable with working directly with our customers."

☐ *Be the business.*   CIOs who have broken the paradox do not think of their role as to support and enable the business; they—and their organizations—simply are the business. Given how hard it is *not* to use the phrase "IT and the business," becoming one with the business takes an awful lot of work. One mistake that Brent Stacey, CIO of Idaho National Laboratory, sees some CIOs make is positioning themselves as something other than a business peer.

"I was grooming a deputy CIO, and he came to me frustrated that he was not getting buy-in from our business executives on our IT strategic plan," says Stacey. "And he was even more frustrated when I told him that he was getting precisely the response he was soliciting." The deputy CIO had been meeting with executives and asking, "How can I help you?" instead of doing some research on a particular business area and talking about plans for improvement.

"When you talk to other executives about the IT strategic plan and the state of the union in IT, how are they going to react?" asks Stacey. "They are going to focus on the things that aren't going right. But if you lead a discussion in the context of that particular executive and talk with him about problem resolution or fundamental process improvement, you will be seen in a different light." In other words, if you want to be treated as a peer of the business, you need to act like a peer of the business. "It is about consciously deciding to be a partner," says Stacey, "not a subordinate. The second you position yourself as a subordinate is the second you brand yourself as a 'boxes and wires' CIO."

☐ *Use the facts.* For something made of wires, bits, and bytes, technology can elicit some fairly strong emotions in the people who attempt to use it. When CEOs are losing thousands of dollars every second the network is down, they tend to get a bit flustered, especially when they have no control over the situation. At Amerisource Bergen, Tom Murphy used heat maps to build a case for infrastructure investments, and at Boeing, Kim Hammonds uses operational efficiency data to keep the company's engineers from developing their own technology. Regardless of the particular approach you take, the more you can lay out the facts and let those facts speak for themselves, the more you can move the conversation from frustration and blame to plans and solutions.

☐ *Cultivate patience.* As we've discussed throughout the book, CIOs have a bias for action; they are change agents who are deadline oriented, and they want results. Their teams are champing at the bit to get moving, and their business partners are hungry, too. As Colleen Wolf, CIO of Ventura Foods, told us, "Projects are won or lost at the beginning. CIOs are in a hurry to demonstrate value.

Especially when they come in as the new CIO, they know that they are under the gun, so they initiate projects that should not be initiated by IT. They get out over their skis."

And as CBRE's Don Goldstein reminds us in the Global Paradox chapter, "Just by saying that we are moving to a global strategy doesn't make it so," he says. "You can lull yourself into a false sense of security by assuming that if the CEO says 'global' and makes you the global CIO that all of a sudden, you can build a global organization."

CIOs who have broken the paradox understand that one of the most evolved of all executive traits is the ability to be patient, the ability to balance the need for speed with the patience to set things up correctly and the courage to gently remind their business partners to cool their jets.

☐ *Be a leader.*   How can you write an entire book about CIOs and not carve out a section on leadership? In the end, whether we are talking about building teams or engaging with business leaders or innovating or setting a vision for the future, we are talking about leadership. CIOs who struggle with establishing credibility at the executive table are CIOs who have not learned how to lead. "CIOs have to make a choice between being a manager and being a leader," says Brent Stacey. "Management is a career and leadership is a calling. If you are a leader, you treat your team as volunteers who commit to the extra effort because they believe in your vision."

If that vision is clear and compelling enough, your team will understand their role in making the vision a reality. If they don't, you will wind up in the weeds. "As a leader, you cannot be involved in the day-to-day management of work. If your team is unclear about your vision and their role in it, they will roll routine decisions up to the next level," says Stacey. "If, as CIO, you are fielding questions about day-to-day transactions, you are probably still a manager."

☐ *Be resilient.*   For Kim Hammonds, CIO of Boeing, one of the most critical skills that she has developed over the years is resilience.

"There are always operational challenges, there are always cost challenges, there are always security challenges, there are always business innovations," she says. "The CIO job is not an easy one, and you have to be able to rebound from difficult situations."

☐ *Be courageous.* Mike Capone, CIO of ADP, has found that one key to breaking the paradox is the ability to tell it like it is. "I am not afraid to kill something early, even if we've already spent a few million dollars," he says. "I stop it and we eat it. I don't measure us by the amount of technology we do." Or as another CIO put it, "Personal courage is critical to CIO success and it shows up in a variety of ways, from hiring talented people and not being threatened by them to articulating a set of convictions even when you know people will not love them to taking on uncomfortable personnel issues. You have to be brave if you are going to influence people. I would rather be fired for speaking out than for failing to speak up."

☐ *Be a business model innovator.* We've hit this one so many times during this book, I'll just touch on it lightly now. For each major evolution in the IT arena, CIOs have had to pick up different skills. The next frontier for technology-driven productivity lies in business model innovation. From construction to financial services to retail to health care, CIOs who are breaking the paradox are no longer content with improving the way their companies do business, they are changing the business at a much more fundamental level.

☐ *Establish transparency.* If I did a word cloud of my interviews for this book, the word "transparency" would be front and center. Here's a paradox for you: if you grew up in IT, you are used to keeping most of the details about technology in a black box. Business leaders are not all that interested in how the sausage is made; they just want to eat it. Yet, in order to build credibility, trust, and business engagement, you need to find a way to communicate a great deal about IT.

One of the most common criticisms I hear CEOs voice about the CIOs they have fired is that "IT was a black hole. We never knew why things cost so much and took so long." CIOs often rely on governance structure to provide transparency, but that can backfire when a complex set of meetings and committees functions as more of a shroud than a window. Not only does the business benefit from transparency into IT, CIOs do as well. As one CIO said to me recently, "The business can be quick to blame IT for what, in the end, are really business problems. The more transparency you can establish, the more public you can make accountability. What the business is supposed to do and what IT is supposed to do are known to everyone." In other words, transparency can be a CIO's best friend.

☐ *Lead change.* I cannot imagine a list of CIO skills that does not include change management. In fact, my own article on the topic in *CIO* magazine in 2007 put change management at the top of the list. In that article, I noted: "Whether it is business process reengineering, organizational restructuring, or a new strategic direction, change can wreak havoc on a company. Leading through that change is probably the most critical skill a CIO can possess."

Jody Davids, then CIO of Cardinal Health, put it this way: "Change management is the skill my staff, my peers, and my manager all value in me the most. And it is the skill I've worked the hardest to build. Our company is changing all the time, so I need to keep the IT organization moving forward."

When driving change, ADP's Mike Capone suggests you pay close attention to the layers of your organization. "When I started in this role, we had a lot of layers," he says. "We had the perception that IT people weren't good managers, so we gave them two people to manage and had something like eleven layers. We quickly found that too many layers are a major obstacle to decision making." So Capone led a reorganization to eliminate five of those layers; he made the technologists who were not good managers into individual contributors and gave them raises.

"Cultural change takes six months per layer in your organization," says Capone. "If you have eleven layers, you won't live long enough to get anything done."

☐ ***Embed IT into the business.*** Call them business relationship executives, portfolio CIOs, or customer relationship managers. Pull them from the business or groom them in IT. Have them report to you, to the business, or on a dual line. Regardless of the path you take, you need executives who can sit at the intersection between IT and its major customers and deliver. You know you are on the right track when you walk into a business unit meeting, and from the dialogue taking place, you cannot easily distinguish the IT person from everyone else.

As IT organizations move away from the traditionally centralized plan-deliver-run structure and appoint these business relationship managers, it becomes even more important that the company's IT leaders find a way to communicate effectively. When Bill Krivoshik was CIO of insurance giant Marsh & McLennan, he built a technology council that brought together line of business CIOs and other technology leaders. When he joined Time Warner as CIO, he was happy to find that structure already in place. "This is a standing meeting of the senior-most people in the IT organization," he says. "Our monthly meetings are by telepresence, and every four months or so, we meet in person for a day." The CIO Council addresses both strategic and transactional issues. For example, at a strategic level, the CIO Council will review the infrastructure plan for creating a shared service and consolidating data centers. They will also work at the tactical level, approving an exception to a standards driven vendor management process when necessary.

Most CIOs of sprawling enterprises will have a technology council, but some work better than others. So, what is the secret to make the group successful? "The meetings have to be meaningful," says Krivoshik. "In the past, I've been on technology councils where vendors come in and talk about esoteric products," says Krivoshik. "You need the council to talk about meaty topics like what is our sourcing strategy for application support? What are we doing about telecom on a global basis?"

Likewise, you have to have the right people at the table. "You need your senior leaders in the group, and they have to show up," says Krivoshik. "Everyone is busy, but once you start letting your senior leaders delegate the role to their direct reports, the meeting won't work. If you can't have full attendance, and the full attention of your senior team, you need to cancel the meeting."

☐ *Communicate.* "The problem with communication is people think that they have actually communicated," says Brent Stacey, paraphrasing the classic quote by George Bernard Shaw. "Today, people need to hear the same message multiple times and in multiple contexts to internalize it. It is almost like branding." Stacey looks for opportunities at lunch, in executive meetings, in elevator conversations, and in formal presentations to repeat a particular message. He also looks for opportunities for his direct reports to repeat the message. This allows him to spread the message further and faster as his directs become as passionate as he is.

☐ *Simplify.* As Geir Ramleth, CIO of Bechtel, puts it in chapter 1 "In IT, we always come up with complexities and barriers for what we want to do and we overlook the simplest solution." Ramleth uses the motto that Speed = Innovation × Simplicity to communicate to his team that the simpler the organization, the greater its ability to drive change. Ramleth's comments in that same chapter, that 80 percent is often better than 100 percent, also support the simplicity theme, as do Mike Capone's observations that delayering your organization will allow you to drive change. Here's a paradox: CEOs understand what it takes to download an app, so they think IT is easy. When in reality, the more simplicity we seek, the more complicated IT can become. What is the path out of that paradox? The more simplicity you build into your IT organization, the more complexity you can handle.

☐ ***Sell the foundation.*** As Tom Murphy points out in chapter 4, "When people are asked to make a major investment in something that doesn't feel competitive or sexy, they tend to resist." If you cannot sell infrastructure investments, you will always be burdened with legacy. You will layer complexity on top of that legacy in an effort to innovate and, as Murphy puts it, "You will make the mess worse, and your company will find you out." If you have not found a way to convince your stakeholders that foundational investments are the table stakes of apps and business intelligence and innovation, you will get crushed between the Scylla and Charybdis of legacy technologies and business demand.

☐ ***Be accountable.*** Kim Hammonds, CIO of Boeing, sums this one up nicely: "If you say you're going to do something you need to do it. That is the only way to build trust and respect." Or as Leslie Jones, CIO of Motorola Solutions, puts it, "I'm not interested in discussing how hard it was. I'm not interested in discussing where we are on things. I'm not interested in discussing how we did it, because from a business's point of view, that is uninteresting. The only thing worth discussing is the result you produce for the business."

☐ ***Watch your language.*** I publish a CIO interview series, and I always ask my interviewees if they have a motto for their IT organization or if they've changed the name of the department. Sometimes I get a very strong negative reaction to the question because "IT excellence is not about what we call ourselves, it is about delivery and results." I understand that perspective, but I believe these CIOs are failing to realize that language matters. With cloud, mobility, big data, and all the rest of it, we are entering an intense new world of computing, where the IT organization is going to be tested as it has never been tested before. Would the introduction of a motto give your team some focus during what promises to be dizzying times? Would a motto allow you to emphasize the two or three attributes you would like your IT organization to be known for? Language is a powerful tool that doesn't cost very much. Be sure you are making the most of it.

Conclusion

At the very heart of the CIO Paradox is the tension between technology and business. CIOs are always looking for the right balance between the two in their strategies, relationships, organizations, and in the leaders they develop.

As IT and the CIO's role have evolved, that balance has shifted this way and that. Certainly, the general trend has been toward a focus on business acumen over technology expertise. Today, with technology residing directly in the revenue streams of so many companies, the need for business acumen is at an all-time high. But here's the rub: these days—with new hardware choices and new technology platforms and big data and consumerization—IT is more about technology than it has been for decades. (As one Fortune 100 CIO, who manages a team of over 1500 people said to me recently, "I'm right back to thinking about end-user computing!) That seesaw, which has leaned first to technology and then to business, is on the verge of breaking. Both ends carry the same weight. Today, it is all about the business *and* it is all about technology.

What this means is that the CIO Paradox is not disappearing; it is growing stronger. The contradictory forces that define IT are getting more acute, and CIOs will work harder than ever to perform. Those who can rise to the occasion and deliver value in this new world of technology will enjoy career advancement and gratification and innovation and reward the likes of which they have not yet seen. But those who are already struggling with the CIO Paradox will continue to struggle. Do a quick count of the number of breaking the paradox boxes you can check, and you will know where you stand.

For the checked items, be sure you are mentoring your senior team to develop the same strengths. They will need those skills as they grow into their role as future CIO. For the unchecked items, do a gut-check. Is this a skill you have the raw DNA to develop? If it is, find a mentor and get moving. If the skill simply falls outside of your natural abilities, give it some thought. Are you an operational CIO being asked to innovate, when innovation is not your thing? Is meeting with external customers something you have no desire ever to do? If that is the case, then add someone with that skillset to your senior leadership team or find a company where operational skills are needed. There are plenty out there.

To me, the CIO role is simply fascinating: It is rife with so many contradictions that I cannot imagine how anyone could ever be successful in it. And yet, I meet them every day. Yes, the CIO Paradox exists and breaking it is as hard as can be. But the CIOs who do it—or who come very close—have a view of business, technology, customers, markets, and human behavior that is beyond the scope of any other executive. If you can get past the Paradox, chances are, you are in for a good time.

Endnotes

The following quotes are from my previously published columns in *CIO* magazine.

1. Maurizio Laudisa quote from "What Are the Built-in Challenges that Set IT Up for Failure?," January 2010.
2. Most of the sources for this book have titles such as SVP and EVP in addition to CIO. In this book, I am using the same approach as *CIO* magazine's editorial team and including only "CIO" to make the prose more pleasant to read.
3. Daniel Priest quote from "Moving Past Old Technology to New Value," May 2011.
4. Jeanne Ross quote from "Busting CIO Myths," May 2012.
5. Greg Carmichael quotes from "Mind the Gap," April 2007.
6. Michael Capellas quote from "Advice for Aspiring CEOs," October 2007.
7. Michael Curran quote from "Advice for Aspiring CEOs," October 2007.
8. Chris Lofgren quote from "Advice for Aspiring CEOs," October 2007.
9. Marc West quote from "Show your CEO the Money," July 2007.
10. Sean O'Neill quote from "Running Your own Technology Company," November 2008.
11. Peter High quote from "Tomorrow's Leadership Skills," June 2012.
12. Jody Davids quote from "New Year, New You," January 2007.

Index

About the Author

Martha and her team at Heller Search Associates specialize in recruiting CIOs and other IT executives across multiple industries. Prior to founding Heller Search, Martha was Managing Director of the IT Leadership Practice at ZRG Partners, a global executive search firm.

Before she established her career in executive search, Martha was Founder and Managing Director of *CIO* magazine's CIO Executive Council, a professional organization for CIOs. Martha also launched and directed the CIO Best Practice Exchange, a members-only network of CIOs from top-tier organizations. During her seven-year tenure at *CIO* magazine, Martha wrote a weekly column on IT leadership and led a series of executive events on IT staffing, career development, and leadership. Before *CIO*, Martha was an editor at Rutgers University Press.

Martha continues to engage with executive audiences. She is *CIO* magazine's CIO Paradox columnist, author of CIO.com's Movers & Shakers blog and author of *You and Your CIO*, a blog on CFO.com. Martha has presented on "the CIO career" at *CIO* events, the CIO Executive Summit, MIT's emerging technology conference, SIM, the United Nations Forum on Women and Technology, and numerous academic executive programs. Martha is also a judge for *CIO* magazine's prestigious CIO 100 Awards.

Martha received her B.A. in English from Hamilton College and her M.A. in English from SUNY Stony Brook. She lives in the Boston area with her husband, two children, and two dogs.